Praise for Le

After th

"Marvelous. . . . [A] tale of human frailty, political machinations and, ultimately, faith. . . . [Hazleton] manages the not inconsiderable feat of maintaining scholarly respect for her subject while also showing a real fondness for the people at the story's heart—people who, we learn, were not unlike us, and whose tale is directly linked to today's newscast."
—*The Dallas Morning News*

"Hazleton not only recounts the facts behind the split but also expertly uses centuries-old accounts to convey the depth of emotional and spiritual associations bundled within a simple word like 'Karbala.' . . . [She] deftly uses original sources, many based on contemporaneous or nearly so oral accounts, to give life and breath to figures familiar to every Muslim but unknown to most non-Muslims."
—*The Seattle Times*

"A remarkable and respectful telling of the story of Islam—a tale of power, intrigue, rivalry, jealousy, assassination, manipulation, greed, and faith that would have made Machiavelli shudder (had he read it), but above all it is a very human story, told in a wonderfully novelistic style that puts most other, often dreary, explanations of the Shia-Sunni divide to shame."
—Hooman Majd, author of *The Ayatollah Begs to Differ*

"A page-turner that reads like an incredible cross between a suspense thriller and a fairy tale. All the elements of a fantastic story are here: intense spirituality; murder, violence, and bloodshed; dynastic power struggles; poison and atrocities; wife murdering husband; slave killing caliph; inspiring heroes; dastardly villains; heresy and apostasy. . . . The implications of [*After the Prophet*] are huge. . . . A superbly written first step for the uninformed to become knowledgeable. Don't miss it."
—*The Free Lance-Star*

Lesley Hazleton

After the Prophet

British-born Lesley Hazleton is a veteran Middle East journalist whose work has appeared in the *New York Times*, *Esquire*, *Vanity Fair*, the *Nation*, and other publications. The author of several books on Middle East politics, religion, and history, she now lives in Seattle, Washington.

www.aftertheprophet.com

Hazleton blogs about religion and politics at
www.accidentaltheologist.com.

ALSO BY LESLEY HAZLETON

Jezebel: The Untold Story of the Bible's Harlot Queen
Mary: A Flesh-and-Blood Biography of the Virgin Mother
Jerusalem, Jerusalem: A Memoir of War and Peace, Passion and Politics
Where Mountains Roar: A Personal Report from the Sinai Desert
Israeli Women: The Reality Behind the Myths

After
the Prophet

The Epic Story of
the Shia-Sunni Split in Islam

Lesley Hazleton

Anchor Books

A Division of Random House, Inc.

New York

FIRST ANCHOR BOOKS EDITION, SEPTEMBER 2010

Copyright © 2009 by Lesley Hazleton

All rights reserved. Published in the United States by Anchor Books,
a division of Random House, Inc., New York, and in Canada
by Random House of Canada Limited, Toronto. Originally
published in hardcover in the United States by Doubleday,
a division of Random House, Inc., New York, in 2009.

Anchor Books and colophon are registered trademarks
of Random House, Inc.

The Library of Congress has cataloged the Doubleday edition as follows:
Hazleton, Lesley, 1945–
After the prophet : the epic story of the Shia-Sunni split in Islam /
Lesley Hazleton.—1st ed.
p.   cm.
Includes bibliographical references and index.
1. Islam—History. 2. Caliphate—History. 3. Muhammad, Prophet,
d. 632—Death and burial. 4. 'A'ishah, ca. 614–678. 5. 'Ali ibn Abi Talib,
Caliph, 600 (ca.)–661. 6. Shi'ah—Relations—Sunnites.
7. Sunnites—Relations—Shi'ah. I. Title.
BP55H42 2009
297.8'04209—dc22
2009006498

Anchor ISBN: 978-0-385-52394-3

Author photograph © Lesly Wiener
Map designed by Jeffrey L. Ward

www.anchorbooks.com

Printed in the United States of America
10   9

Contents

Note on
Usage and Spelling

Throughout this book, I have used first names for major figures rather than full names, in order to avoid the "Russian novel effect," where English readers suffer the confusion of multiple unfamiliar names. Thus, for instance, I have used Ali instead of Ali ibn Abu Talib, Aisha instead of Aisha bint Abu Bakr, Omar instead of Omar ibn al-Khattab, and so on. I have used fuller names only where there is a risk of confusion; thus, the son of the first Caliph, Abu Bakr, is referred to as Muhammad Abu Bakr, itself abbreviated from Muhammad ibn Abu Bakr.

I have used the spelling "Quran" instead of the more familiar English rendering "Koran" for the sake of both accuracy and consistency, and in order to respect the difference between the Arabic letters *qaf* and *kaf*. Otherwise, wherever possible, I have used more familiar English spellings for the names of major figures (Othman, for instance, instead of Uthman or Uttman, and Omar instead of Umar) and have purposely omitted diacritical marks, using Shia rather than Shi'a, Ibn Saad instead of Ibn Sa'd, Muawiya instead of Mu'awiya, Quran instead of Qur'an.

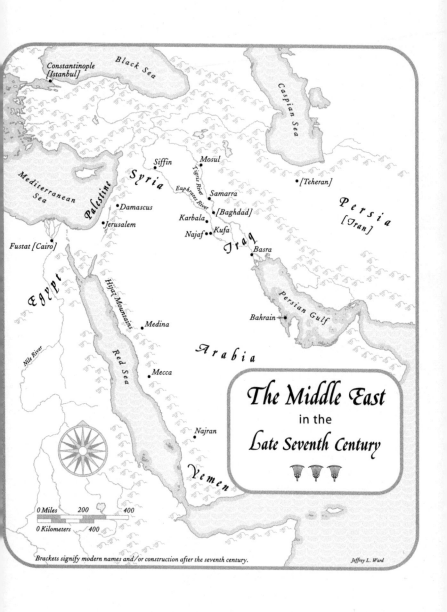

Constantinople
[Istanbul]

Black Sea

Caspian Sea

Mediterranean
Sea

Syria

Palestine

Siffin

Mosul

Tigris River

Euphrates River

Samarra

[Teheran]

Persia
[Iran]

Damascus

Karbala

[Baghdad]

Jerusalem

Najaf

Kufa

Iraq

Basra

Fustat [Cairo]

Egypt

Nile River

Hijaz Mountains

Persian Gulf

Bahrain

Medina

Red Sea

Arabia

Mecca

The Middle East
in the
Late Seventh Century

Najran

0 Miles   200   400

0 Kilometers   400

Yemen

Brackets signify modern names and/or construction after the seventh century.

Jeffrey L. Ward

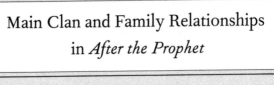

Main Clan and Family Relationships
in *After the Prophet*

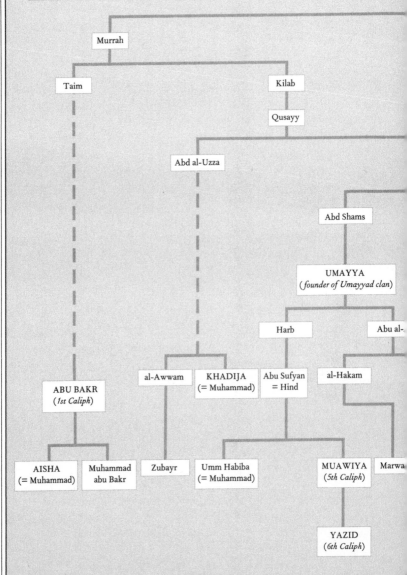

Murrah

Taim

Kilab

Qusayy

Abd al-Uzza

Abd Shams

UMAYYA
(*founder of Umayyad clan*)

Harb

Abu al-

ABU BAKR
(*1st Caliph*)

al-Awwam

KHADIJA
(= Muhammad)

Abu Sufyan
= Hind

al-Hakam

AISHA
(= Muhammad)

Muhammad
abu Bakr

Zubayr

Umm Habiba
(= Muhammad)

MUAWIYA
(*5th Caliph*)

Marwa

YAZID
(*6th Caliph*)

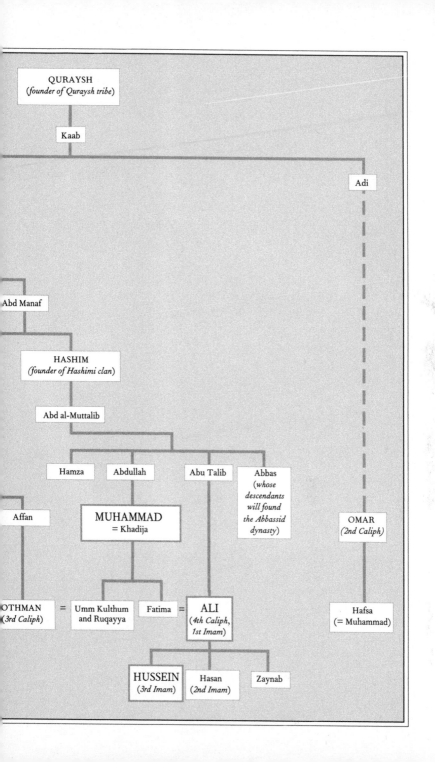

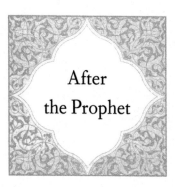

After
the Prophet

Prologue

THE SHOCK WAVE WAS DEAFENING. IN THE FIRST FEW SECONDS after the blast, the millions of pilgrims were rooted to the spot. Everyone knew what had happened, yet none seemed able to acknowledge it, as though it were too much for the mind to process. And then as their ears began to recover, the screaming began.

They ran, panicked, out of the square and into the alleys leading to the gold-domed mosque. Ran from the smoke and the debris, from the blood and shattered glass, the severed limbs and battered bodies. They sought security in small, enclosed spaces, a security obliterated by the next blast, and then the next, and the next.

There were nine explosions in all, thirty minutes of car bombs, suicide bombs, grenades, and mortar fire. Then there was just the terrible stench of burned flesh and singed dust, and the shrieking of ambulance sirens.

It was midmorning on March 4, 2004—the tenth of Muharram in the Muslim calendar, the day known as Ashura. The city of Karbala was packed with Shia pilgrims, many of whom had journeyed on foot the fifty miles from Baghdad. They carried huge banners billowing above their heads as they chanted and beat their chests in ritualized mourning for the Prince of Martyrs, Muhammad's grandson Hussein, who was killed in this very place. Yet there was an air of celebration too. The mass pilgrimage had been banned for years; this was the first time since the fall of the Saddam regime that they had been able to mourn proudly and openly, and their mourning was an expression of newfound freedom. But now, in a horrible reverse mirror of the past, they too had been transformed into martyrs.

The Ashura Massacre, they would call it—the first major sign of the civil war to come. And on everyone's lips, the question, How had it come to this?

The Sunni extremist group Al Qaida in Iraq had calculated the attack with particularly cruel precision. When and where it took place were as shocking as the many hundreds of dead and wounded. Ashura is the most solemn date in the Shia calendar—the equivalent of Yom Kippur or Easter Sunday—and the name of Karbala speaks of what happened on this day, in this place, in the year 680. It is a combination of two words in Arabic: *karab,* meaning destruction or devastation, and *bala,* meaning tribulation or distress.

Muhammad had been dead not fifty years when his closest male descendants were massacred here and the women of his family taken captive and chained. As word of the massacre spread, the whole of the Muslim world at the time, from the borders of India in the east to Algeria in the west, was in shock, and the question they asked then was the same one that would be asked fourteen centuries later: How had it come to this?

What happened at Karbala in the seventh century is the foundation story of the Sunni-Shia split. Told in vivid and intimate detail in the earliest Islamic histories, it is known to all Sunnis throughout the Middle East and all but engraved on the heart of every Shia. It has not just endured but gathered emotive force to become an ever-widening spiral in which past and present, faith and politics, personal identity and national redemption are inextricably intertwined.

"Every day is Ashura," the Shia say, "and every place is Karbala." And on March 4, 2004, the message was reiterated with terrifying literalness. The Karbala story is indeed one without end, still unfolding throughout the Muslim world, and most bloodily of all in Iraq, the cradle of Shia Islam.

This is how it happened, and why it is still happening.

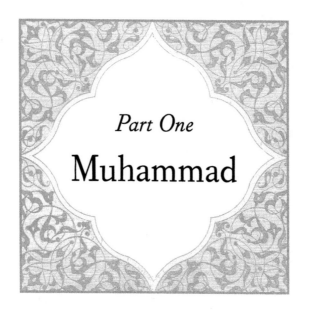

Part One

Muhammad

chapter 1

I<small>F THERE WAS A SINGLE MOMENT IT ALL BEGAN, IT WAS THAT OF</small> Muhammad's death. Even the Prophet was mortal. That was the problem. It was as though nobody had considered the possibility that he might die, not even Muhammad himself.

Did he know he was dying? He surely must have. So too those around him, yet nobody seemed able to acknowledge it, and this was a strange blindness on their part. Muhammad was sixty-three years old, after all, a long life for his time. He had been wounded several times in battle and had survived no fewer than three assassination attempts that we know of. Perhaps those closest to him could not conceive of a mere illness bringing him down after such concerted malice against him, especially now that Arabia was united under the banner of Islam.

The very people who had once opposed Muhammad and plotted to kill him were now among his senior aides. Peace had been made, the community united. It wasn't just the dawn of a new age; it was morning, the sun bright, the day full of promise. Arabia was poised to step out of the background as a political and cultural backwater and take a major role on the world stage. How could its leader die on the verge of such success? Yet dying he definitely was, and after all the violence he had seen—the battles, the assassination attempts—he was dying of natural causes.

The fever had begun innocuously enough, along with mild aches and pains. Nothing unusual, it seemed, except that it did not pass. It came and went, but each time it returned, it seemed worse. The symptoms and duration—ten days—seem to indicate bacterial meningitis, doubtless contracted on one of his military campaigns and, even today, often fatal.

Soon blinding headaches and wrenching muscle pain weakened him so much that he could no longer stand without help. He began to drift in and out of sweat-soaked semiconsciousness—not the radiant trance in which he had received the Quranic revelations but a very different, utterly debilitating state of being. His wives wrapped his head in cloths soaked in cold water, hoping to draw out the pain and reduce the fever, but if there was any relief, it was only temporary. The headaches grew worse, the throbbing pain incapacitating.

At his request, they had taken him to the chamber of Aisha, his favorite wife. It was one of nine built for the wives against the eastern wall of the mosque compound, and in keeping with the early ethic of Islam—simplicity, no inequalities of wealth, all equal as believers—it was really no more than a one-room hut. The rough stone walls were covered over with reed roofing; the door and windows opened out to the courtyard of the mosque. Furnishings were minimal: rugs on the floor and a raised stone bench at the back for the bedding, which was rolled up each morning and spread out again each night. Now, however, the bedding remained spread out.

It was certainly stifling in that small room even for someone in full health, for this was June, the time when the desert heat builds to a terrible intensity by midday. Muhammad must have struggled for each breath. Worst of all, along with the headaches came a painful sensitivity to noise and light. The light could be dealt with: a rug hung over the windows, the heavy curtain over the doorway kept down. But quiet was not to be had.

A sickroom in the Middle East then, as now, was a gathering place. Relatives, companions, aides, supporters—all those who scrambled to claim closeness to the center of the newly powerful religion—came in a continual stream, day and night, with their concerns, their advice, their questions. Muhammad fought for consciousness. However sick, he could not ignore them; too much depended on him.

Outside, in the courtyard of the mosque, people were camped out, keeping vigil. They refused to believe that this illness could be anything but a passing trial, yet they were in a terrible dilemma, for they had seen too many people die of just such sickness. They knew what was likely to happen, even as they denied it. So they prayed and they waited, and the sound of their prayers and concern built to a constant, unrelenting hum of anxiety. Petitioners, followers, the faithful and the pious, all wanted to be where news of the Prophet's progress would be heard first—news that would then spread by word of mouth from one village to another along the eight-mile-long oasis of Medina, and from there onto the long road south to Mecca.

But in the last few days, as the illness worsened, even that steady murmur grew hushed. The whole of the oasis was subdued, faced with the inconceivable. And hovering in the air, on everyone's mind but on nobody's lips, at least in public, was the one question never asked out loud. If the impossible happened, if Muhammad died, who would succeed him? Who would take over? Who would lead?

It might all have been simple enough if Muhammad had had sons. Even one son. Though there was no strict custom of a leader's power passing on to his firstborn son at death—he could always decide on a younger son or another close relative instead—the eldest son was traditionally the successor if there was no clear statement to the contrary. Muhammad, however, had neither sons nor a designated heir. He was dying intestate—*abtar*, in the Arabic, meaning literally curtailed, cut off, severed. Without male offspring.

If a son had existed, perhaps the whole history of Islam would have been different. The discord, the civil war, the rival caliphates, the split between Sunni and Shia—all might have been averted. But though Muhammad's first wife, Khadija, had given birth to two sons alongside four daughters, both had died in infancy, and though Muhammad had married nine more wives after her death, not one had become pregnant.

There was surely talk about that in Medina, and in Mecca too. Most of the nine marriages after Khadija had been political; as was the custom among all rulers of the time, they were diplomatic alliances. Muhammad had chosen his wives carefully in order to bind the new community of Islam together, creating ties of kinship across tribes and across old hostilities. Just two years earlier, when Mecca had finally accepted Islam and his leadership, he had even married Umm Habiba, whose father had led Mecca's long and bitter opposition to him. But marital alliances were sealed by children. Mixed blood was new blood, free of the old divisions. For a leader, this was the crucial point of marriage.

Most of Muhammad's wives after Khadija did indeed have children, but not by him. With the sole exception of the youngest, Aisha, they were divorcées or widows, and their children were by previous husbands. There was nothing unusual in this. Wealthy men could have up to four wives at the same time, with Muhammad allowed more in order to meet that need for political alliance, but women also often had two, three, or even four husbands. The difference was that where the men had many wives simultaneously, the women married serially, either because of divorce—women divorced as easily as men at the time—or because their previous husbands had died, often in battle.

This meant that the whole of Mecca and Medina was a vast interlocking web of kinship. Half brothers and half sisters, in-laws and cousins, everyone at the center of Islam was related at least three or four different ways to everyone else. The result beggars the modern Western idea of family. In seventh-century Arabia, it was a far-reaching web of relationships that defied anything so neatly linear as a family tree. It was more of a dense forest of vines, each one spreading out tendrils that then curled around others only to fold back in on themselves and reach out again in yet more directions, binding together the members of the new Islamic community in an intricate matrix of relationship no matter which tribe or clan they had been born into. But still, blood mattered.

There were rumors that there was in fact one child born to Muhammad after Khadija—born to Mariya the Copt, an Egyptian slave whom Muhammad had freed and kept as a concubine, away from the mosque compound—and that indeed, the child had been a boy, named Ibrahim, the Arabic for Abraham. But unlike the ancestor for whom he was named, this boy never grew to adulthood. At seventeen months old, he died, and it remains unclear if he ever actually existed or if, in a culture in which sons were considered a sign of their fathers' virility, he was instead a kind of legendary assurance of the Prophet's honor.

Certainly any of the wives crowded around Muhammad's sickbed would have given her eyeteeth—all her teeth, in fact—to have had children by him. To have been the mother of his children would have automatically granted her higher status than any of the other wives. And to bear the son of the Prophet? His natural heir? There could be no greater honor. So every one of them surely did her utmost to become pregnant by him, and none more than Aisha, the first wife he had married after the death of Khadija.

The youngest of the nine, the favorite, and by far the most controversial, Aisha was haunted by her childlessness. Like the others, she must certainly have tried, but in vain. Perhaps it was a sign of Muhammad's ultimate loyalty to the memory of Khadija, the woman who had held him in her arms when he was in shock, trembling from his first encounter with the divine—the first revelation of the Quran—and assured him that he was indeed *Rasul Allah*, the Messenger of God. Perhaps only Khadija could be the matriarch, and only her eldest daughter, Fatima, could be the mother of Muhammad's treasured grandsons, Hasan and Hussein.

There can be no question of impotence or sterility on Muhammad's part; his children by Khadija were proof of that. No question either of barrenness on the part of the later wives, since all except Aisha had children by previous husbands. Perhaps, then, the multiply married Prophet was celibate. Or as Sunni theologians would argue in centuries to come, perhaps this late-life childlessness was the price of revelation. The Quran was the last and final word of God, they said. There could be no more prophets after Muhammad, no male kin who could assert special insight or closeness to the divine will, as the Shia would claim. This is why Khadija's two infant boys had to die; they could not live lest they inherit the prophetic gene.

All we know for sure is that in all nine marriages after Khadija, there was not a single pregnancy, let alone a son, and this was a major problem.

Muhammad was the man who had imposed his will—the will of God—on the whole of the vast Arabian Peninsula. He had done it in a mere two decades, since the angel Gabriel's first appearance to him. *Iqra*, "recite," the angel had told him, and thus the stirring opening lines of the Quran—"the Recitation"—came into being. Further revelations had come steadily, and in the most beautiful Arabic anyone had ever heard, transcendent poetry that was taken as a guarantee of its divine origin, since surely no illiterate trader like Muhammad was capable of creating such soul-stirring beauty on his own. He was literally the Messenger, the man who carried the revealed word of God.

As Islam spread through the towns, oases, and nomadic tribes of Arabia, they had all prospered. The accrued wealth of taxes and tribute was now that of the Islamic community as a whole. But with a public treasury and publicly owned lands, it was all the more important that their leader leave a will—that he designate his successor or at least establish clear guidelines for how his successor was to be determined.

What did he intend to happen after his death? This is the question that will haunt the whole tragic story of the Sunni-Shia split, though by its nature, it is unanswerable. In everything that was to follow, everyone claimed to have insight into what the Prophet thought and what he wanted. Yet in the lack of a clear and unequivocal designation of his successor, nobody could prove it beyond any shadow of doubt. However convinced they may have been that they were right, there were always those who would maintain otherwise. Certainty was a matter of faith rather than fact.

It is clear that Muhammad knew that he would die, if not quite yet. He had no illusions of his own immortality. True, he was still full of vitality—his gait had been strong until the illness struck, his build solid and muscular, and only a close observer could have counted the few white strands in what was still a full head of dark, braided hair—but those three assassination attempts must have made him more aware than most that his life could be cut short. On the other hand, a close brush with death is sometimes the renewed impetus for life. Indeed, the most serious of those attempts to kill him had been a major turning point in the establishment of Islam.

That had been ten years earlier, when his preaching had so threatened the aristocrats of his native Mecca. His message was a radical one, aimed above all at the inequities of urban life, for despite the prevailing image of seventh-century Arabia as nomadic, most of its population had been settled for several generations. Social identity was still tribal, however; your status was determined by what tribe you were born into, and no tribe was wealthier or more powerful than the Quraysh, the urban elite of Mecca.

The Quraysh were merchant traders, their city a central point on the north-south trade route that ran the length of western Arabia. It had become so central less because of any geographical advantage—if anything, it involved a slight detour—than because it was home to the Kaaba. This cube-shaped shrine housed numerous regional deities, many of them said to be offspring of a higher, more remote deity known simply as Allah, "*the* God." Mecca was thus a major pilgrimage center, and since intertribal rivalries were suspended within its walls during pilgrimage months, it also provided a safe venue for large trading fairs.

This combination of pilgrimage and commerce proved highly profitable. The Quraysh skillfully melded faith and finance, charging fees for access to the Kaaba, tolls on trade caravans, and taxes on commercial transactions. But the wealth they generated was not shared by all. The traditional tribal principle of caring for all its members had not survived the passage into urban life, so that while some clans within the tribe prospered, others did not. It was these others with whom Muhammad's message would first resonate.

The poor, the orphaned, the enslaved—all were equal in the eyes of God, Muhammad taught. What tribe you were born to, what clan within that tribe, what household within that clan—none of this mattered. No one group had the right to raise itself up above others. To be Muslim—literally to submit yourself to God's will—was to forsake all the old divisiveness. It meant no more tribe against tribe or rich against poor. They were one people, one community, bound together in the simple but stunning acknowledgment that there was no god but God.

It was an egalitarian message, as revolutionary in its time and place as that of an earlier prophet in first-century Palestine. And to those who controlled the city's wealth, it was downright subversive, a direct challenge to the status quo of power. As Muhammad's following increased, the Meccan elite had done all they could to silence him, but everything they tried, from vilification to boycott, had failed. Finally, a group of leading Meccans, one from every major clan of the Quraysh, banded together in the dark outside Muhammad's house, knives at the ready, waiting for him to emerge for dawn prayers. Warned of the plot just in time, he fled Mecca under cover of night along with a single companion and headed for the oasis city of Medina to the north, where he was welcomed first as a peacemaker between feuding tribes, then as a leader. The year of his nighttime flight for refuge—the *hijra*, or emigration—would become the foundation year of the Islamic calendar: 622 A.D., or the year One A.H., After the Hijra.

Under Muhammad, the oasis city became the political center of Arabia, threatening to eclipse Mecca to the south. The power struggle between the two cities would include two major battles and countless skirmishes, but eight years after forcing Muhammad out, Mecca had finally accepted his leadership. The *fatah*, they would call it, the "opening" of the city to Islam. The Kaaba had been rededicated to the one God, Allah, and Muhammad had acted on his message of unity by reaching across the aisle, as it were, and welcoming many of the Meccan elite into the leadership of Islam.

Friends could be as dangerous as long-term enemies, though. Muhammad certainly knew that assassination could also be used by those closest to you. Throughout the world of the time, it had long been a prime pathway to power. Appoint your successor, and that appointee, no matter how trusted, might always be tempted to speed up events, to preempt the natural life cycle by artificial means. A carefully crafted poison in a honeyed drink or a dish of succulent lamb? Such things were not unknown. In fact, they were soon to become all too familiar.

But what is most likely is that Muhammad knew that the moment he formally appointed a successor, he would be introducing divisiveness into the newly united community of Islam—or, rather, feeding into the divisiveness that already existed. He would set in motion the web of resentments and jealousies that had accumulated as people jockeyed for influence and position, as they will around any man of charisma, let alone a prophet. However hard he may have tried to smooth them over, disagreements that had merely simmered beneath the surface would become all too visible. Factions would form, arguments develop, his whole life's work teeter on the edge of collapse. Perhaps that was inevitable, and he simply could not bring himself to endorse the inevitable. He had put an end to intertribal warfare; he had empowered the powerless; he had overthrown the old aristocracy of Mecca, expelled the old pagan gods, and founded the world's third great monotheistic faith. He had achieved what had seemed the impossible, but could the impossible survive him?

There are signs that Muhammad was all too aware of what would happen after his death. One tradition has it that his last words were: "Oh God, have pity on those who succeed me." But then what did he mean by that? Was it an expression of humility? Or perhaps an invocation to the one God to help his people? Or did Muhammad, with his final breath, foresee the terrible saga of blood and tears to come? There is no way of knowing. As the old Arabic saying has it, "Only God knows for sure." Words are always subject to interpretation. Thoughts can only be imagined, and that is the work of novelists. We have to rely on the basic stuff of history, the accounts of those who were there. And each one had his or her own angle, his or her own interest in the outcome.

Sunni scholars would argue in centuries to come that Muhammad had such faith in the goodwill and integrity of all Muslims that he trusted to them, and to God, to ensure that the right decision be made. He saw the community itself as sacred, these scholars would argue, meaning that any decision it made would be the correct one. But Shia scholars would maintain that Muhammad had long before made the divinely guided choice of his closest male relative—his son-in-law Ali—as his successor. He had done so many times, in public, they would say, and if Ali's enemies had not thwarted the Prophet's will, he would certainly have done so again, one last time, as he lay dying in that small chamber alongside the mosque.

In those ten final days of Muhammad's life, everyone who plays a major role in this story was in and out of that sickroom, in particular one woman and five men, each of them a relative, and each with a direct interest in the matter of who would succeed the Prophet. The men included two of his fathers-in-law, two of his sons-in-law, and a brother-in-law, and indeed all five would eventually succeed him, claiming the title of Caliph—the *khalifa,* or successor, of Muhammad. But how that would happen, and in what order, would be the stuff of discord and division for fourteen centuries to come.

Whatever divisions may have existed between the men as Muhammad lay dying, however, they paled compared with that between Aisha, the childless favorite whose room they were in, and Ali, the youngest of the five men. As Muhammad's first cousin and his adopted son as well as his son-in-law, he was the Prophet's nearest male relative. Yet Aisha and Ali, the two people closest of all to Muhammad on a daily basis, had barely been able to speak a civil word to each other for years, even in his presence.

The tension between the two surely made the air in that sickroom all the more stifling, yet it seemed that not even the Prophet could foresee how their mutual animosity would determine the future of Islam. After all, how could something as seemingly small as a necklace lost seven years earlier have set the scene for the centuries of division that lay ahead?

chapter 2

It was not just any necklace, though it would have been easy enough to think so, for it was really no more than a string of beads. They may have been agates, or coral, or even simple seashells—Aisha never did say, and one can almost see her waving her hand dismissively, as though such detail were irrelevant. Perhaps she was right, and it's enough to know that it was the kind of necklace a young girl would wear, and treasure more than if it had been made of diamonds because it had been Muhammad's gift to her on her wedding day.

Its loss and the ensuing scandal would be known as the Affair of the Necklace, the kind of folksy title that speaks of oral history, which is how all history began before the age of the printing press and mass literacy. The People of the Cloak, the Episode of Pen and Paper, the Battle of the Camel, the Secret Letter, the Night of Shrieking—all these and more would be the building blocks of early Islamic history. This is history told as story, which of course it always is, but rarely in such vivid and intimate detail.

For the first hundred years of Islam, these stories lived not on the page but on the tongues of those who told them and in the ears and hearts of those who heard them and remembered them to tell again, the details gathering impact as the years unfolded. This was the raw material of the early Islamic historians, who would travel throughout the Middle East to gather these memories, taking great care to record the source of each one by detailing the chain of communication. The *isnad*, they called it—the provenance of each memory—given up front by prefacing each speaker's account in the manner of "I was told this by C, who was told it by B, who was told it by A, who was there when it happened."

This was the method used by Ibn Ishaq in his biography of Muhammad; by Abu Jafar al-Tabari in his magisterial history of early Islam, which comes to thirty-nine volumes in English translation; by Ibn Saad in his sometimes deliciously gossipy collections of anecdotes; and by al-Baladhuri in his "Lineage of the Nobles." It is an extraordinarily open process, one that allows direct insight into how history is communicated and established, and is deeply respectful of the fact that, *Rashomon* style, if there were six people there, they would have six similar but subtly different accounts.

Al-Tabari was Sunni, but his vast history is acknowledged as authoritative by Sunni and Shia alike. Its length and detail are part and parcel of his method. He visits the same events again and again, almost obsessively, as different people tell their versions, and the differing versions overlap and diverge in what now seems astonishingly postmodern fashion. Al-Tabari understood that human truth is always flawed—that realities are multiple and that everyone has some degree of bias. The closest one might come to objectivity would be in the aggregate, which is why he so often concludes a disputed episode with that time-honored phrase "Only God knows for sure."

Reading these voices from the seventh century, you feel as though you are sitting in the middle of a vast desert grapevine, a dense network of intimate knowledge defying the limitations of space and time. As they relate what they saw and what they heard, what this one said and how that one replied, their language is sometimes shocking in its pithiness—

not at all what one expects from conventional history. It has the smack of vitality, of real people living in earthshaking times, and it is true to the culture, one in which the language of curse was as rich and developed as the language of blessing. Indeed, both curse and blessing figure prominently in what is to come.

The necklace was lost just one day's journey outside Medina, toward the end of one of Muhammad's campaigns to unite Arabia's tribes under the banner of Islam. These were full-scale expeditions lasting weeks and even months at a time, and he usually took at least one of his wives along with him. None was more eager to go than Aisha.

For a spirited city teenager, this was pure excitement. If Medina was not yet a city in the way we now think of the word—it was more of an agglomeration of tribal villages, each one clustered around a fortified manor house—it was urban enough for the nomadic past to have become a matter of nostalgia. Long poems celebrated the purity of the desert, softening its harshness with the idea of a spiritual nobility lost in the relative ease of settled life.

For Aisha, then, these expeditions were romance. There was the thrill of riding out of the ribbon of green that was Medina, up into the jagged starkness of the mountains that rose like a forbidding no-go zone between Medina and the vast deserts of central and northern Arabia. The Hijaz, they called it—the "barrier"—and beyond it stretched more than seven hundred miles of arid steppe until the land suddenly dipped into the lush river basin of the place they knew as al-Iraq, from the Persian word for lowlands.

This was Aisha's chance to discover the fabled purity of the desert, and she must have savored every detail of it, admiring the way the scouts who led them knew where every spring was, hidden deep between clefts of rock, every place where a well had been sunk, every dip in the landscape that held the sudden winter rains to create pools that would vanish within a few days. They needed no compasses, no maps; the land was in their heads. They were master travelers.

From her vantage point in her howdah—a canopied cane platform built out from the camel's saddle—Aisha saw the vast herds of the camel and horse breeders in the northern steppes; the date palm oases of Khaybar and Fadak nestled like elongated emeralds in winding valleys; the gold and silver mines that produced much of the wealth of the Hijaz; the Beduin warriors of remote tribes, fiercely romantic to a city girl. She watched and listened to the drawn-out negotiations with those tribes that resisted acknowledging Muhammad and Islam, hoping for a peaceful outcome even as some other part of her may have hoped the talks would break down so that the only choice left was the sword and the world devolved into action, men's voices grown hoarse with yelling and the air charged with the clang of steel and the acrid tang of blood.

It was on these expeditions that she learned her repertoire of battle cries, spurring on the men from the rear. The women of seventh-century Arabia were no shrinking violets, and least of all Aisha, known for her sharp tongue and her wit. She learned to curse the enemy, to praise her own side's virility, to urge the men on to new feats of valor as she would do years later in the thick of battle, even as men were dying all around her. She knew her invective was unnerving, all the more powerful—eerie, almost—for coming in the high, shrill, piercing voice she was known for, unmistakably hers. But both her tongue and her wit would almost fail her now.

It had still been dark when they began to break camp to start the final leg of the journey home, using the cool early hours of the day to advantage. In the chilly predawn half-light, Aisha made her way a hundred yards or so beyond the encampment to relieve herself behind a spindly bush of broom, as women still do when they're out in the wild, looking for a modicum of privacy. She got back to her camel just as the caravan was preparing to move off, and had already settled into the howdah when she put her fingers to her throat and her heart skipped a beat—that sudden sense of something missing, of absence where there should have been presence. Her necklace, her gift from Muhammad, was gone.

She realized instantly what must have happened. The string had snagged on a branch and snapped without her noticing, scattering the beads onto the ground. But if she was quick about it, there was still time to retrieve them. Without a word to anyone, she slipped down from the howdah and retraced her steps.

Even for someone so determined, though, finding the beads took longer than she'd foreseen. In the early half-light, every broom bush looked the same, and when she finally found the right one and knelt down, she had to sift through the piles of dead needles beneath the bush to find each bead. Yet find them she did, one by one, and returned triumphantly to the camp with the beads tied securely into a knot in the hem of her smock, only to discover that the camp was no longer there. The whole expedition had moved on, and she was suddenly alone in the desert.

How it had happened was understandable. Her maid, an Ethiopian slave girl, had seen her climbing into the howdah, but nobody had seen her slip out again. They had all assumed she was inside and that since the canopy was drawn, she did not want to be disturbed, so they had left without her. What was not quite as understandable to most people was what happened next, or rather, what did not happen next.

Aisha did not run after the caravan, even though the well-trodden route was clear enough. She did not even walk after it, though it could not have been far ahead. Camels laden with equipment and supplies do not move fast. It would have been easy to catch up on foot, especially in the early morning before the sun has gained heat, when the chill of the desert night still hangs in the air, crisp and refreshing—a matter of an hour or so at the most.

Instead, in her own words, "I wrapped myself in my smock and then lay down where I was, knowing that when I was missed they would come back for me."

It was inconceivable to Aisha that her absence would not be noted, unthinkable that the caravan would not halt and a detachment be sent back to find her. As the Prophet's wife she assumed a position of privilege. To expect her to catch up on foot was to expect her to behave like a normal teenage girl, and if there was one thing she would insist on all her life, it was her exceptionality.

There was the age at which she had married Muhammad, to start with. She had been a mere child, she later maintained: six years old when she was betrothed to him and nine years old when the marriage was celebrated and consummated. And though this was unlikely, few disputed her claim in her lifetime. Indeed, few people cared to dispute with her at all. As one of the most powerful Caliphs would say many years later, "There was never any subject I wished closed that she would not open, or that I wished open that she would not close."

But if Aisha was indeed married so young, others would certainly have remarked on it at the time. In fact most reports have her aged nine when she was betrothed and twelve when she was actually married, since custom dictated that girls not marry until puberty. But then again, to have been married at the customary age would have made Aisha normal, and that was the one thing she was always determined not to be.

As she reminded everyone who would listen through to the end of her life—an enviably long one compared to the other main figures in this story since she would outlive them all—she was not only Muhammad's youngest wife but also the purest, the only one who had been neither a divorcée nor a widow but a virgin at marriage. And most important of all, she was Muhammad's favorite.

Humayra—"my little redhead"—he called her, though she was almost certainly not a natural redhead. If she had been, it would have led to much comment in dark-haired Arabia; indeed she herself, never shy with words, would have said a lot more about it. But a double measure of henna would have made her hair glow dark red, as was of course the purpose. It emphasized her difference.

She had been the first of the nine wives Muhammad had married after the death of Khadija—offered by her father, Muhammad's close friend and longtime supporter Abu Bakr, as a means of distracting the Prophet in the depth of his mourning. It was easy to see why. Bold and irrepressible, she would bring him back to life. By her own account, at least, she would tease and taunt him and not only get away with it but be loved for it. Muhammad seemed to have granted her license for girlish mischief, as though he were a fond father indulging a spoiled daughter, entranced by her sassiness and charm.

Charming she must have been, and sassy she definitely was. Sometimes, though, the charm wears thin, at least to the modern ear. The stories Aisha later told of her marriage were intended to show her influence and spiritedness, but there is often a definite edge to them, a sense of a young woman not to be crossed or denied, of someone who could all too easily switch from spirited to mean-spirited.

There was the time Muhammad spent too long for Aisha's liking with another wife, who had made a "honeyed drink" for him—a kind of Arabian syllabub, probably, made with egg whites and goat's milk beaten thick with honey, for which Muhammad had a particular weakness. When he finally came to her chamber and told her why he had been delayed, she made a face and, knowing that he was particular about bad breath, wrinkled her nose in distaste. "The bees that made that honey must have been eating wormwood," she insisted, and was rewarded when the next time Muhammad was offered a honeyed drink, he refused it.

Other times she went further, as when Muhammad arranged to seal an alliance with a major Christian tribe newly converted to Islam by marrying its leader's daughter, a girl renowned for her beauty. When the bride-to-be arrived in Medina, Aisha volunteered to help prepare her for the wedding and, under the guise of sisterly advice, advised her that Muhammad would think all the more highly of her if on the wedding night, she resisted him by saying, "I take refuge with God from thee." The new bride had no idea that this was the Islamic phrase used to annul a marriage. All she knew was that the moment she said it, Muhammad left, and the next day she was bundled unceremoniously back to her own people.

Aisha, in short, was used to having things her own way, so when she was left behind in the desert, she saw no reason to expect anything different. If there was the slightest murmur of panic at the back of her mind as the sun rose higher overhead and she took shelter under a scraggly acacia tree, as the shadow of the tree grew shorter and still nobody came, she would never have acknowledged it, not even to herself. Of course she would be missed. Of course someone would be sent for her. The last thing anyone would expect was that she, the favorite wife of the Prophet, run after a pack of camels like some Beduin shepherd girl. That would be just too demeaning.

Someone did come, though not a special contingent deputized to search for her, as she had expected. In fact the expedition sent nobody at all, since they never realized she was missing, not even after they had reached Medina. In the hubbub of arrival—the hundreds of camels being unloaded and stabled, the throng of warriors being greeted by wives and kinsmen—her absence went unnoticed. Her maid assumed she'd slipped down from the howdah and gone perhaps to see her mother. Muhammad himself would have been far too busy to think of her. Everyone simply assumed she was someplace else.

So it was Aisha's good fortune, or perhaps her misfortune, that a certain young Medinan warrior had been delayed and was riding alone through the heat of the day to catch up with the main expeditionary force when he saw her lying under that acacia tree.

His name was Safwan, and in what Aisha would swear was an act of chivalry as pure as the desert itself, he recognized her immediately, dismounted, helped her up onto his camel, then led the animal on foot the whole twenty miles to Medina. That was how everyone in the oasis witnessed the arrival of the Prophet's wife just before nightfall, hours behind the main body of the expedition, sitting tall and proud on a camel led by a good-looking young warrior.

She must surely have sensed that something was wrong as people stared in a kind of stunned astonishment. Must have noticed how they hung back, with nobody rushing up to say, "Thanks be to God that you're safe." Must have seen how they looked sideways at each other and muttered as she passed. No matter how upright she sat on Safwan's camel, how high she held her head or how disdainful her glare, she must have heard the tongues start to wag as children ran ahead, spreading the word, and must have known what that word was.

The sight was too much to resist. The Prophet's youngest wife traveling alone with a virile young warrior, parading through the series of villages strung along the valley of Medina? Word of it ran through the oasis in a matter of hours. A necklace indeed, people clucked. What could one expect of a childless teenager married to a man in his late fifties? Alone the whole day in the desert with a young warrior? Why had she simply lain down and waited when she could have caught up with the expedition on foot? Had it been a prearranged tryst? Had the Prophet been deceived by his spirited favorite?

Whether anyone actually believed such a thing was beside the point. In the seventh century as today, scandal is its own reward, especially when it has a sexual aspect. But more important, this one fed into the existing political landscape of the oasis. What Aisha and Safwan may or may not have done in the desert was not really the issue. This was about Muhammad's reputation, his political standing.

Any slur on Aisha was a slur on her whole family, but especially on the two men closest to her: the man who had given her in marriage and the man who had taken her. Her father, Abu Bakr, had been Muhammad's sole companion on that night flight from Mecca for the shelter of Medina, and that distinction had helped make him one of the leading figures among the former Meccans who had made Medina the new power center of Arabia. The Emigrants, they were called, and right there in the name was the fact that the Medinans still thought of them as foreign, as Meccans. They were respected, certainly, but not quite accepted. They still had that whiff of outsiders who had come in and somehow taken over, as though the Medinans themselves had not invited them. So it was the native Medinans, the ones known as the Helpers, who were especially delighted by this new development. In the politics of seventh-century Medina, as anywhere in the world today, the appearance of impropriety was as bad as impropriety itself.

Even among the Emigrants, though, there were those who thought the Abu Bakr household needed to be taken down a peg, and especially the young girl who so evidently thought herself better than anyone aside from the Prophet himself. Among the women in particular, Aisha was resented. Muhammad's daughters, let alone his other wives, were weary of her grandstanding. For the first time, the young girl so insistent on standing out, on being exceptional, found herself standing out too much.

There is no doubt that Aisha was innocent of the charges against her. She may have been young and headstrong, but she also had a highly developed sense of politics. To risk her whole standing, let alone her father's, for a passing dalliance? That was out of the question. The favorite wife of the Prophet consorting with a mere warrior, and one who wasn't even from one of the best families? She would never dream of it.

Safwan had behaved as she had expected him to behave, the white knight to her maiden in distress. To imply anything beyond that was the most scurrilous slander. How could anyone even think such a thing?

Certainly Muhammad did not. If anything, he must have felt guilty about having left his young favorite alone in the desert, so at first he dismissed the rumors, convinced that they would die down soon enough. But in this he seriously misread the mood of the oasis.

Overnight, the poets got busy. They were the gossip columnists, the op-ed writers, the bloggers, the entertainers of the time, and the poems they wrote now were not lyrical odes, but the other great form of traditional Arabic poetry: satires. Laced with puns and double enten-dres, they were irresistibly repeatable, building up momentum the more they spread. The barbed rhyming couplets acted like lances, verbal at-tacks all the more powerful in a society where alliances were made on a promise and a handshake, and men were literally taken at their word.

Soon the whole oasis was caught up in a fervor of sneering insinu-ation. At the wells, in the walled vegetable gardens, in the date orchards, in the inns and the markets and the stables, even in the mosque itself, up and down the eight-mile length of the Medina valley, people reveled, as people always have and always will, in the delicious details, real or imag-ined, of scandal.

Try as he might, Muhammad could no longer ignore the matter. That Aisha was innocent was not the point; she had to be *seen* as inno-cent. He was well aware that his power and leadership were not beyond dispute in Medina, while to the south Mecca still remained in opposition to him and, even after two major battles, would not submit for another five years. The scurrilous satirical poems had already reached that mer-chant city, where they were received with outright glee.

Muhammad had been placed in a double bind. If he divorced Aisha, he would by implication be acknowledging that he had been de-ceived. If he took her back, he risked being seen as a doting old man bamboozled by a mere slip of a girl. Either way, it would erode not only his own authority as the leader of Medina but the authority of Islam itself. Incredible as it seemed, the future of the new faith seemed to hang on a teenage girl's reputation.

In the meantime, he banished Aisha from her chamber on the eastern wall of the mosque courtyard and sent her home to Abu Bakr. There she was kept indoors, away from prying eyes and ears, while word was put out that she had returned to her father's house to recuperate from a sudden illness. Not that the rumormongers were buying it. Illness, indeed, they said knowingly; she was hiding her face in shame, as well she might.

For the first time in her life, nothing Aisha could say—and as one early historian put it, "she said plenty"—could make any difference. She tried high indignation, wounded pride, fury against the slander, but none of it seemed to have any effect. Years later, still haunted by the episode, she even maintained that Safwan was known to be impotent—that "he never touched women"—an unassailable statement since by then Safwan was long dead, killed in battle, and so could not defend his virility.

A teenage girl under a cloud, Aisha finally did what any teenage girl would do. She cried. And if there was a touch of hyperbole to her account of those tears, that was understandable under the circumstances. As she put it later, "I could not stop crying until I thought the weeping would burst my liver."

You could say it was just chance that the loss of a necklace should create such trouble. You could point to it, as conservative Muslim clerics still do, as an example of what happens when women refuse to stay home and instead take an active part in public life. You could counter that this is just the same old sexist trick of blaming the woman in the story. Or you could argue that it was inevitable that trouble begin with Aisha, given her personality and, above all, given her resentment of Muhammad's first wife.

The wealthy merchant widow Muhammad had married when she was forty and he twenty-five, Khadija was the woman to whom he had been faithful, in a monogamous marriage, until the day she died. It had been in her arms that he had sought shelter and comfort from the awe and terror of revelation, her voice that had reassured him and confirmed the awesome validity of his mission. No matter how many more times he married, he would never find that quality of love again.

How could a teenage girl possibly compete against the hallowed memory of a dead woman? But then who but a teenage girl would even dream of trying?

"I wasn't jealous of any of the Prophet's wives except for Khadija, even though I came after her death," she said many years later. And though this was clearly untrue—whenever there was so much as a mention of another wife's beauty, Aisha bristled—Khadija was certainly the focus of her jealousy. Muhammad's first wife was the one woman who, precisely because she was dead, was unassailable. He had made this perfectly clear, for in all of Aisha's teasing of him, the one time she went too far—the one time Muhammad rebuked her—was when she dared turn that sharp tongue of hers on Khadija.

It took the form of a question designed, it seemed, to taunt Muhammad with her own attractiveness. It was the kind of question only a teenager could ask and only an older woman could regret as she related the incident many years later. In language unmistakably hers—nobody else would have dared be so startlingly direct—the young Aisha had asked Muhammad how he could possibly remain so devoted to the memory of "that toothless old woman whom God has replaced with a better."

You can see how she intended this as a flirtatious tease, blithely unaware of the effect of her words. But the fact remains that they were said with the casual disregard of the young and vivacious for the old and dead, the cruel derision of a teenager. And if Aisha thought for a moment she could gain precedence over Khadija in such a way, Muhammad's response stopped her in her tracks.

"Indeed no, God has not replaced her with a better," he said. And then, driving the point home: "God granted me her children while withholding those of other women."

There it was: Not only was Khadija the only one beyond all criticism, but the Prophet himself held Aisha's childlessness against her. A virgin bride she may have been, but in a society where women gained status through motherhood, mother she was not and would never be.

Is that where her determination began, or had it been there all along? For determination was what it would take for Aisha to remake herself as she did. This childless teenager would establish herself after the Prophet's death as the leader of the Mothers of the Faithful, the term by which his widows were known. She would be the one who spoke for them all, who would transform herself into *the* Mother of the Faithful, a power behind the throne whose approval was sought by every ruler and whose influence was underestimated by none. Mother of none, she would become—at least as she saw it—the mother of all Muslims.

Daring, headstrong, outspoken even when it reflected badly on herself, Aisha stands squarely at the center of this story, able to run verbal rings around every man in it. Every man, that is, but one, and that was the man to whom Muhammad now turned for advice in the Affair of the Necklace.

chapter 3

IF THERE WAS A SINGLE PERSON WHO SEEMED DESTINED TO BE Muhammad's successor, it was Ali, his first cousin and the man whose name the Shia were to take as their own. They were, and are, the followers of Ali, or in Arabic, *Shiat Ali*—Shia, for short.

Ali had been the first man to accept the new faith of Islam. He'd been only thirteen years old at the time, yet he'd remember it with the kind of absolute clarity that marks the most momentous points of one's life. It had happened just after Muhammad's first soul-shaking encounter with the angel Gabriel. Still caught up in the utter terror of a human who had come face-to-face with the divine, he had sought refuge in Khadija's arms, and once she had reassured him—"This truly is an angel and not a devil, and you will be the prophet of this people"—he had called together his closest kinsmen and asked for their support. "Which of you will assist me in this cause?" he asked.

As Ali would tell it, "They all held back from this, while I, although I was the youngest of them, the most diseased in eyesight, the most corpulent in body and thinnest in the legs, said 'I, oh Prophet of God, will be your helper in this matter.' "

Diseased eyes? Corpulent? Thin legs? Was Ali joking at his own expense? His self-description bears no resemblance to the virile yet tender warrior in the brightly colored posters so popular among the Shia faithful, who have little of the Sunni abhorrence of visual representation. On sale in kiosks and from street vendors throughout the Shia heartland, from Lebanon to India, the posters show not an awkward teenager but a handsome man in his forties. The jaw set firm beneath the neatly trimmed beard, the strong eyebrows, the dark eyes raised upward—you might almost mistake his portrait for the conventional image of Christ except that it has more of a sense of physical vitality and strength.

There is the sword for one thing. Sometimes slung over his back, sometimes laid across his lap, this sword was destined to become more famed throughout the Islamic world than King Arthur's sword Excalibur ever would be in Christendom. Like Excalibur, it came with supernatural qualities, and it too had a name: Dhu'l Fikar, the "Split One," which is why it is shown with a forked point, like a snake's tongue. In fact it wasn't the sword that was split but the flesh it came in contact with, so that the name more vividly translates as the Cleaver or the Splitter.

It had been Muhammad's own sword, given by him to Ali—bequeathed, you might say. And after he had fought valiantly in battle with this sword, despite multiple wounds, Ali earned the best known of the many titles Muhammad would confer on him: *Assad Allah*, Lion of God. That is why he is often shown with a magnificently maned lion crouched at his feet, staring out at the viewer with the calm gaze of implacable strength.

The name Lion of God was intended to convey spiritual as well as physical strength, and that is the sense you get from these ubiquitous posters. With his high cheekbones, *kohl*-rimmed eyes, and green *keffiya* artfully draped around his head and falling onto his shoulders—the green of Islam from the banner of Muhammad's clan, the color so evocative of ease and bounty to a mountain desert people—Ali is shown as the perfect Islamic man.

So what if at thirteen he was a shortsighted, spindly-legged adolescent? As Shia Muslims point out, these are not direct portraits but representations. They express the feel of Ali, who he is for them—the man mentored and groomed by Muhammad himself, inducted by the Prophet into the inner, gnostic meaning of Islam so that his understanding of the faith would far surpass that of all others. What does it matter if in life he was not the most handsome man in the world? In spirit is where he lives, stronger in body and in many ways stronger still in influence and respect than when he was alive.

Muhammad seemed to recognize this the moment he heard those first words of unwavering commitment from his young cousin. "He put his arm around my neck," Ali remembered, "and said 'This is my brother, my trustee, and my successor among you, so listen to him and obey.' And then everyone got up and began joking, saying to my father, 'He has ordered you to listen to your son and obey him.' "

It seems clear enough when told this way: not only the designation of Ali as Muhammad's successor but also the first sign of what Islam would mean—the revolutionary upending of the traditional authority of father over son and by implication of the whole of the old established order. No one tribe would lord it over another any longer. No one clan would claim dominance within a tribe, and no one family within a clan. All would be equal in the eyes of the one God, all honored members of the new community of Islam.

Yet from Ali's own account, it was not taken seriously. In fact it is not even clear that it was intended seriously. Ali was still a mere stripling, barely strong enough to wield any sword, let alone Dhu'l Fikar, while Muhammad was a man without his own means, an orphan who had been raised in his uncle's household and whose only claim to wealth was through his wife, Khadija. It made little sense for this seemingly ordinary man, whom his kinsmen had known all their lives, to suddenly declare himself the Messenger of God. The declaration itself must have seemed absurd to many of those who heard it, let alone the idea of appointing a successor. There was, after all, nothing to succeed to. At that moment in time, Islam had only three believers, Muhammad, Khadija, and Ali. How could any rational person imagine that it would develop into a great new faith, into a united Arabia and an empire in the making? Muhammad was a man who appeared to have nothing worth bequeathing.

That was to change over the next two decades. As the equalizing message of Islam spread, as Muhammad's authority grew, as tribe after tribe and town after town officially accepted the faith and paid tribute in the form of taxes, the new *ummah*, the community of Islam, grew not only powerful but wealthy. By the time Muhammad lay dying, nearly the whole of the Arabian Peninsula had allied itself with Islam and its unitary Arab identity, and over those years, time and again, Muhammad had made it clear how close he held Ali, the one man who had had faith in him when all others scoffed.

"I am from Ali and Ali is from me; he is the guardian of every believer after me," he said. Ali was to him "as Aaron was to Moses," he declared. "None but a believer loves Ali, and none but an apostate hates him." And most famously, especially for the mystical Sufis, for whom Ali would become the patron saint of knowledge and insight: "I am the City of Knowledge and Ali is its gateway."

Shia scholars still relate these sayings obsessively as proof of Muhammad's intention that Ali succeed him, yet not one of these later declarations has the absolute clarity of that word "successor." Not one of them clearly said, "This is the man whom I designate to lead you after I die." Always implied, it was never quite stated, so that what seemed incontrovertible proof to some, remained highly ambiguous to others.

One thing was not ambiguous, however. Nobody, Sunni or Shia, denies the extraordinary closeness between Muhammad and Ali. In fact the two men were so close that at the most dangerous point in the Prophet's life, Ali served as Muhammad's double.

That had been when the Meccans had plotted to kill Muhammad on the eve of his flight to Medina. While the would-be assassins lay in wait outside his house for him to emerge at dawn—even in their murderous intent, they obeyed the traditional Arabian injunction barring any attack on a man within the confines of his own home—Ali had arranged for Muhammad to escape along with Abu Bakr, and stayed behind as a decoy. It was Ali who slept that night in Muhammad's house, Ali who dressed in Muhammad's robes that morning, Ali who stepped outside, risking his own life until the assassins realized they had the wrong man. Ali, that is, who for the space of that night stood in for Muhammad and who finally escaped himself to make the long journey to Medina in the humblest possible fashion, alone, on foot.

In a way, it seemed fated that Ali should take on the role of Muhammad's double. Despite the twenty-nine-year age difference between the two cousins, there was a kind of perfect reciprocity in their relationship, for each had found refuge as a boy in the home of the other. After his father's death, the orphaned Muhammad had been raised in his uncle Abu Talib's household, long before Ali was even born, and years later, when Abu Talib fell on hard times financially, Muhammad, by then married to Khadija and running the merchant business she had inherited from her first husband, had taken in his uncle's youngest son as part of his own household. Ali grew up alongside Muhammad's four daughters and became the son Muhammad and Khadija never had. The Prophet became a second father to him, and Khadija a second mother.

Over time, the bonds of kinship between the two men would tighten still further. In fact, they would triple. As if Ali were not close enough by virtue of being Muhammad's paternal first cousin and his adoptive son, Muhammad handpicked him to marry Fatima, his eldest daughter, even though others had already asked for her hand.

Those others were the two men who would lead the challenge to Ali's succession after Muhammad's death: Aisha's father, Abu Bakr, who had been Muhammad's companion on the flight to Medina, and the famed warrior Omar, the man who was to lead Islam out of the Arabian Peninsula and into the whole of the Middle East. But whereas Abu Bakr and Omar had given Muhammad their daughters in marriage, he had refused each of them when they asked for the hand of Fatima. The meaning was clear: in a society where to give was more honorable than to receive, the man who gave his daughter's hand bestowed the higher honor. While Abu Bakr and Omar honored Muhammad by marrying their daughters to him, he did not return the honor but chose Ali instead.

It was a singular distinction, and to show how special he considered this marriage to be, the Prophet not only performed the wedding ceremony himself but laid down one condition: the new couple would follow the example of his own marriage to Khadija and be monogamous. Ali and Fatima, he seemed to be saying, would be the new Muhammad and Khadija, and would have the sons Muhammad and Khadija never had.

Sure enough, the man who remained without sons of his own soon had two adored grandsons, Hasan and Hussein. Only a year apart, they instantly became the apples of their grandfather's eye. It is said that there is no love purer than that of a grandparent for a grandchild, and Muhammad was clearly as doting and proud a grandfather as ever lived. He would bounce the young boys on his lap for hours at a time, kissing and hugging them. Would even happily abandon all the decorum and dignity of his position as the Messenger of God to get down on all fours and let them ride him like a horse, kicking his sides with their heels and shrieking in delight. These two boys were his future—the future of Islam, as the Shia would see it—and by fathering them, Ali, the one man after Muhammad most loyal to Khadija, had made that future possible.

When Khadija died, two years before that fateful night of Muhammad's flight to Medina, Ali had grieved as deeply as Muhammad himself. This was the woman who had raised him as the son she never had, and then became his mother-in-law. Devoted as he was to Muhammad, he had been equally devoted to her. It was clear to him that no matter how many wives the Prophet might take after Khadija's death, none could possibly compare, and least of all the one who seemed the most determined to prove herself superior.

Long before the Affair of the Necklace, then, before those beads went rolling in the desert to set off scandal, Ali remained impervious to Aisha's sassiness and charm. In his eyes, Muhammad's youngest wife must have seemed an unworthy successor to Khadija. And the antipathy was mutual. To her, Ali's devotion to Khadija's memory was a constant reminder of the one rival she could never conquer, while his two sons were daily reproof of her own inability to produce an heir. She, Aisha, was supposed to be the apple of Muhammad's eye, not these two adored grandsons in whom the Prophet seemed to take even more delight than he did in her, and certainly not the drab, modest Fatima, their mother, or the superior Ali, their father, who accorded her none of the deference and respect she was convinced she should command.

That rebuke of Muhammad's for her criticism of Khadija had hit Aisha hard, and since she was not the forgiving type, let alone the forgetting one, the impact of the blow did not lessen with time. If anything, it increased. Banned from any further criticism of Khadija, and unable to compete on the most basic yet most important level—the continuation of the bloodline—she displaced her resentment onto the one person who seemed safe, Khadija's eldest daughter.

Fatima had none of the robust health and vitality of Aisha. Fifteen years older, she was frail by comparison, almost sickly. She could not make her father laugh with paternal affection as Aisha did, could not tease him, could barely even gain his ear unless it was to do with her sons. Her place had been taken by Aisha, who effectively set about shutting her out. More daughter than wife, Aisha saw herself as competing with Fatima for Muhammad's affection, and in such a competition, Fatima stood no chance.

It became known throughout Medina that if you wanted a favor from Muhammad, the best time to approach him was after he had been with Aisha because then he was guaranteed to be in a good mood. The young wife had influence, and in one way or another, she used it in a barrage of small slights and insults that Fatima was helpless to counter. Things came to a head when Muhammad's other wives begged Fatima to go to her father and protest against his favoritism of Aisha. She felt she had no choice but to comply yet must have known that in doing so, she would be setting herself up for humiliation. And indeed, the moment she broached the subject, Muhammad stopped her short.

"Dear little daughter," he said, "do you not love who I love?"

To which Fatima could only meekly reply, "Yes, surely."

His question was rhetorical, of course, and though it was phrased in loving terms, you can almost hear the impatience in his voice, the desire to put a stop to this constant bickering among those close to him and have them leave him alone to get on with important matters of state. But he also seemed to be saying that his love for Aisha trumped his love for everyone else.

That is certainly what Ali heard when his wife came home in tears of shame; the insult was not only to Fatima but also to him, and, worst of all, to Khadija. He immediately sought out Muhammad and confronted him, calling him to account for neglecting his blood family. "Was it not enough for you that Aisha should have insulted us," he said, "but then you tell Fatima that Aisha is your best beloved?" And while the Prophet may have been able to ignore Fatima, he could not ignore Ali. He would now make amends.

He chose the occasion well. The long arm of the Byzantine Empire had reached deep into Arabia, and the town of Najran, midway on the main trade route between Mecca and the Yemen to the south, was the largest center of Christianity in the peninsula. The Quranic message spoke powerfully to Arabian Christians, as it did to several of the Jewish tribes that had fled south from Palestine after failed rebellions against Roman rule centuries before, and that were by now all but indistinguishable in language and culture from their Arab neighbors. Islam was based, after all, on the religion of Abraham. It was widely believed that the Kaaba had originally been built by Adam and then rebuilt by Abraham, and that the Arabs were the descendants of Abraham's son Ishmael. Islam was seen less as a rejection of existing faiths than as an elevation of them into a new, specifically Arabian identity.

Yet Najran was divided. Those in favor of accepting Islam argued that Muhammad was clearly the Paraclete or Comforter whose arrival Jesus had foretold in the Gospels. Those against maintained that since the Paraclete was said to have sons, and Muhammad had no son, it could not possibly be he. Finally they decided to send a delegation to Medina to resolve the matter directly with Muhammad in the time-honored manner of public debate. But Muhammad preempted the need for debate. In a piece of consummate theatricality, he came out to meet the delegation without his usual bevy of counselors. Instead, only his blood family were with him: Ali and Fatima, and their sons, Hasan and Hussein.

He didn't say a word. Instead, slowly and deliberately, in full view of all, he took hold of the hem of his cloak and spread it high and wide so that it covered the heads of his small family. They were the ones he sheltered under his cloak, he was saying. They were the ones he wrapped around himself. They were his nearest and dearest, the *Ahl al-Bayt,* the People of the House of Muhammad—or as the Shia would later call them, the People of the Cloak.

It was a brilliantly calculated gesture. Arabian Christian tradition had it that Adam had received a vision of a brilliant light surrounded by four other lights and had been told by God that these were his prophetic descendants. Muhammad had certainly heard of this tradition and knew that the moment the Najran Christians saw him spread his cloak over the four members of his family, they would be convinced that he was another Adam, the one whose coming Jesus had prophesied. Indeed, they accepted Islam on the spot.

But Muhammad's gesture with the cloak also spoke to Ali and Fatima. There were ties of love and ties of blood, he was saying, and between the two, blood must always come first. There was no room for the childless Aisha under that cloak.

It was only to be expected that Muhammad would turn to Ali for advice on how to proceed in the Affair of the Necklace, but from Aisha's point of view, he could not have consulted a worse person. Indeed—at least by her account, which is the only one we have—Ali's advice could hardly have been more blunt. Surprisingly blunt, in fact, since Ali was known for his eloquence. The collection of his speeches and sermons known as *Nahj al-Balagha*, or the Path of Eloquence, would be taught for centuries as the exemplar of perfection in language and spirit. Famed for his depth and his insight, he would represent the ideal combination of warrior and scholar, courage and chivalry. But at least according to Aisha, there was no hint of chivalry, let alone eloquence, in the advice he now gave.

Perhaps he made a far more sophisticated argument, and Aisha gave only the gist of it. Perhaps he had lost patience with the melodramatic aspect of the whole business, or perhaps he could simply take no more of Aisha. All we know for certain is that while the advice he gave Muhammad might be seen by some as refreshingly forthright, it also seems peculiarly curt.

"There are many women like her," he said. "God has freed you from constraints. She is easily replaced." There are plenty more fish in the sea, that is. Divorce her and be rid of the whole affair.

It was the first open expression of the crack in the newly formed bedrock of Islam—the jagged break, barely perceptible at first, that would develop into a major fault line. The casual dismissiveness of Ali's words, the barely concealed contempt, didn't just sting but cut to the bone. Yet the casualness is precisely what makes it so humanly persuasive. That throwaway phrasing, that evident disdain, that apparent willingness to believe in Aisha's infidelity—all this she would hold against him as long as she lived.

There is no record of whatever else Ali may have advised, though he almost certainly said more. Not only is the curtness of his response strangely uncharacteristic, but so too is the fact that it failed to take into account Muhammad's dilemma. Divorcing Aisha would solve nothing, for the rumors of infidelity would still stand unchallenged, eroding Muhammad's authority. Resolution could come only by grace of a higher authority, which was exactly what now happened.

After three weeks of indecision, Muhammad went to Abu Bakr's house to question Aisha himself. There, even as she swore her innocence yet again, he went into a prophetic trance. As she would tell it, "The Prophet was wrapped in his garment and a leather cushion was put under his head. . . . Then he recovered and sat up and drops of water fell from him like rain on a winter day, and he began to wipe the sweat from his brow, saying, 'Good news, Aisha! God has sent down word of your innocence.' "

It was a divine revelation, perfectly timed. That same day Muhammad proclaimed it in public, in the words that are now part of Sura 24 of the Quran: "The slanderers were a small group among you, and shall be punished. But why, when you heard it, did faithful men and women not think the best and say, 'This is a manifest lie'? If the slanderers had even produced four witnesses! But they produced no witnesses, so they are liars in the eyes of God. . . . Why did you think nothing of repeating what others with no knowledge had said, thinking it a light matter when in the eyes of God it was a serious one? Why did you not say, 'This is a monstrous slander'? God commands the faithful never to do such a thing again."

It was a glorious exoneration of Aisha, and all the more powerful in that it demanded not one but all of four people to contradict her word.

Unless there were four witnesses to an illegal sexual act, it said, the accused was blameless, and the false accusers were the ones to be punished.

For a wronged woman, there could have been no better outcome, yet the form of it would be cruelly turned around and used by conservative clerics in centuries to come to do the opposite of what Muhammad had originally intended: not to exonerate a woman but to blame her. The wording of his revelation would apply not only when adultery was suspected but also when there had been an accusation of rape. Unless a woman could produce four witnesses to her rape—a virtual impossibility—she would be considered guilty of slander and adultery, and punished accordingly. Aisha's exoneration was destined to become the basis for the silencing, humiliation, and even execution of countless women after her.

She had no idea that this would be the case, of course. What she knew was that the accusations against her had been declared false, and by no less than divine authority. Her accusers were publicly flogged in punishment, and the poets who had composed the most scurrilous verses against her were now suddenly moved to compose new ones in lavish praise of her. She returned to her chamber in the courtyard of the mosque and resumed her role as the favorite wife, though now with the added status of being not only the sole person in whose presence Muhammad had received a revelation but also the only one to have had a revelation specifically about her.

Nevertheless, she paid a price. The days of her freedom to join Muhammad's campaigns were over. With the exception of the pilgrimage to Mecca, she would not travel those desert routes again for as long as Muhammad lived. She must certainly have missed the adventure of those expeditions, perhaps also the guilty thrill of being so close to warfare. Fearless, even reckless, she would have made a fine warrior, but it would be all of twenty-five years until she would see battle again.

There was another price too, though again, Aisha had no way of knowing the full extent of it. The sight of her riding into Medina on Safwan's camel had branded itself into the collective memory of the oasis, and that was the last thing Muhammad needed. In due course, another Quranic revelation dictated that from now on, his wives were to be protected by a thin muslin curtain from the prying eyes of any men not their kin. And since curtains could work only indoors, they would soon shrink into a kind of minicurtain for outdoors: the veil.

The Revelation of the Curtain clearly applied only to the Prophet's wives, but this in itself gave the veil high status. Over the next few decades it would be adopted by women of the new Islamic aristocracy—and would eventually be enforced by Islamic fundamentalists convinced that it should apply to all women. There can be little doubt that this would have outraged Aisha. One can imagine her shocking Muslim conservatives by tearing off her veil in indignation. She had accepted it as a mark of distinction—but as an attempt to force her into the background? The girl so used to high visibility had no intention of being rendered invisible.

Meanwhile, if Muhammad had ever doubted her, it was easy to forgive him, but not Ali. Even as Muhammad lay dying seven years later, the events that would eventually place Aisha at the head of an army against Ali had already been set in motion. That advice he had given the Prophet would rankle throughout her life. Indeed, it rankles still today. *Al-Mubra'a,* the Exonerated, Sunnis still call her, but some Shia would use a different title for her, one that by no coincidence rhymes with her name: *Al-Fahisha,* the Whore.

chapter 4

THE SEEDS OF DIVISION HAD BEEN SOWN. MUHAMMAD'S WIVES, fathers-in-law, sons-in-law, cousins, daughters, aides, closest companions—everyone would be drawn into it as the seeds took root. But as Muhammad lay dying, it was the wives who were in control. It was they who guarded the sickroom, who determined if he was well enough to receive visitors or so weak that even the closest companions should be turned away; they who had argued about whose chamber he should be taken to until he insisted that it be Aisha's; and they who now argued over which medicine to give him, even about whether to give him any medicine at all.

As the life slowly seeped out of the Prophet, the disputes increased over who should be allowed in to see him and who not. The few times he mustered the strength to make it clear exactly whom he wanted to see, they argued also about that. Even as he was helpless to prevent it, the dying man could see his worst fears coming true.

There was the time when he called for Ali, who spent most of those days studying and praying in the mosque, but Aisha lobbied instead for her father. "Wouldn't you rather see Abu Bakr?" she said. Her cowife Hafsa countered by suggesting her own father. "Wouldn't you rather see Omar?" she asked. Overwhelmed by their insistence, Muhammad waved assent. Both Abu Bakr and Omar were called for; Ali was not.

Cajoling a mortally sick man into doing as they wanted may seem unbecoming, even heartless, but who could blame these young wives for pushing their own agenda, for promoting the interests of their fathers over those of other possible successors like Ali? They faced a daunting future, and they knew it.

They were about to be widowed, and widowed forever. They were fated, that is, to become professional widows. It was right there in the revelation that would be part of Sura 33 of the Quran. "The Prophet is closer to the Faithful than their own selves, and his wives are their mothers," it said. "You must not speak ill of the Messenger of God, nor shall you ever wed his wives after him. This would surely be a great offense in the eyes of God."

If the Prophet's wives were indeed the Mothers of the Faithful, to marry any of them even after his death would be tantamount to incest.

This ban on remarriage went against the grain of custom. In seventh-century Arabia, widows were remarried almost immediately, often to a relative of the dead husband, so that the family would be preserved and protected. To forbid this was surely a striking exception to Muhammad's forceful advocacy for the care of widows and orphans and the needy. But then that was the point: the wives were exceptional. The ban on their remarrying emphasized the idea of the Islamic community as one large family.

While this may have worked well enough for the older wives, it must have seemed at best ironic, at worst even cruel, to the youngest of them. Aisha would be a lifetime mother, even as by the same stroke of revelation, she would be denied the chance ever to become pregnant and give birth to children of her own.

Certainly there would have been no shortage of suitors for any of Muhammad's wives. Men would have vied to marry a widow of the Messenger of God, gaining political advantage by claiming closeness to him in this way. Indeed, that may be exactly what he sought to prevent. It was not as though the idea had not already occurred to some. Aisha's ambitious cousin Talha had once been heard to say out loud that he wanted to marry her after Muhammad's death—a desire that resulted in his quickly being married off to one of her sisters instead. But the word of revelation had since forestalled any more such ambitions, and that word was final. Muhammad would leave behind nine widows, and not one would ever marry again.

None of them could have been more anxious about her future than Aisha. At barely twenty-one, she was about to become the lifetime widow of a man who had not even made a will. Would she have to go back to her father's house and live out her life in a kind of premature retirement? The very idea of retirement at so young an age might have been daunting for even the most reclusive of women; for Aisha, it must have been horrifying. Used to being at the center of attention, she was not about to be relegated to the sidelines. Yet if Ali were to be designated Muhammad's successor in a deathbed declaration, she feared this was exactly what would happen. She could expect nothing good from that, and neither could her father, Abu Bakr, who had been as deeply wounded as she herself had been by Ali's role in the Affair of the Necklace.

Ali's blunt advice had been a slur on Abu Bakr's honor and that of his whole family—indeed, on all the Emigrants. That is certainly how Omar saw it. He and Abu Bakr were the two most senior of Muhammad's advisers; close friends, both were fathers-in-law of the Prophet, despite being younger than he—Abu Bakr by two years, Omar by twelve. But where the stooped, white-haired Abu Bakr inspired affection and reverence, Omar, the stern military commander, seemed to inspire something closer to fear.

In that small sickroom, he must have been an overwhelming presence. So tall that Aisha would say that "he towered above the crowd as though he were on horseback," Omar was always with a riding crop in his hand and always ready to use it, on man or beast. His voice was the voice of command; honed to terseness on the battlefield, it compelled obedience. The moment he came into any room, Aisha would remember, all laughter stopped. People's voices trailed off into silence as they registered his arrival; faces turned toward him as they waited for him to speak. There was no room for small talk around Omar, no space for frivolity. His presence now at the side of the ailing Prophet was a confirmation of how serious the situation had become.

Every person in that room wanted to safeguard Islam, yet each also wanted to safeguard his or her own position. As is the way in political matters, all were convinced that the interests of the community and their own personal interests were one and the same. And all this could be sensed in the strange and disturbing incident that came to be known as the Episode of Pen and Paper.

On the ninth day of Muhammad's illness, he appeared to recover somewhat—the kind of illusory improvement that often precedes the end. He seemed perfectly lucid as he sat up, sipped some water, and made what many believe was one final attempt to make his wishes known. But even this came laden with ambiguity.

"Bring me writing materials that I may write something for you, after which you will not be led into error," he said.

It seems a simple enough request and a perfectly reasonable one under the circumstances, but it produced near panic among those in the room at the time: the wives, Omar, and Abu Bakr. Nobody there knew what it was Muhammad wanted to write—or rather, as tradition has it, to dictate to a scribe, since one of the basic tenets of Islam is that he could neither read nor write, however improbable that may have been in a man who was for many years a merchant trader. That would have required that he keep records of what was bought and sold, and though this was no great literary art, it did require the basic skills of literacy. But Muhammad's assumed illiteracy acted as a kind of guarantee that the Quran had been revealed, not invented, that it was truly the word of the divine, not the result of human authorship.

Whether the dying Prophet wanted to write or to dictate, though, the question now on everyone's mind was the same: What would it be? General guidelines for how they should proceed? Religious advice to the community he was about to leave behind? Or the one possibility that seemed most called for and yet was most feared: a will. Was the dying Prophet about to definitively name his heir?

The only way to know was to call for the pen and paper to be brought to him, but that is not what happened. No sooner had he uttered the request than everyone attending him was aware of what it might mean. What if it really was to write his will? What if it was not in their favor? What if it named Ali as his successor, not Abu Bakr or Omar or another of his close companions? And if it was indeed his will he wanted to write, why not simply speak it? Why insist on pen and paper? Did that mean that even on his deathbed, he did not trust them to carry it out and so wanted it written down, unambiguously, for all to see?

None of this did anyone there say out loud, however. Instead, they voiced concern about overstraining Muhammad in his illness. They worried about placing too much pressure on him. They argued that the sickroom should be kept quiet, and even as they stressed the need for silence, their voices rose.

It is the strangest scene. There was every sign that the man they were all so devoted to was ready to make his dying wishes known, perhaps even designate his heir, once and for all. It was the one thing everyone wanted to know, and, at the same time, the one thing nobody wanted to know. If Ali turned out to be the designated heir, nobody in that room wanted it put into writing.

Yet it is also an altogether human scene. Everyone so concerned, everyone crowded around, trying to protect Muhammad from the importuning of others, to ease life for a mortally ill man. They were all, it seemed, doing their best. But as their voices rose in debate over the pros and cons of calling for pen and paper, the terrible sensitivity to noise overtook Muhammad again. Every angry note, every high-pitched syllable seemed to drill through his brain like an instrument of torture until he could take it no more. "Leave me," he said finally. "Let there be no quarreling in my presence."

He was so weak by then that the words came out in a mere murmur. Only Omar managed to hear him, but that was enough. Using his commanding presence to full advantage, he laid down the law. "The Messenger of God is overcome by pain," he said. "We have the Quran, the Book of God, and that is sufficient for us."

It would not be sufficient, though. It could have been and perhaps should have been—Omar's words are still used today as the model of perfect faith—but it was not. The Quran would be supplemented by the practice of Muhammad, his example in everything from the greatest events to the smallest details of everyday life, as related by those closest to him. The *sunna*, it would be called—the traditional Arabian word for the custom or tradition of one's forefathers—and this was the word from which the Sunnis would eventually take their name, though the Shia would follow nearly all the same traditions.

In the meantime, Omar's argument prevailed. His words had their intended effect, and the sickroom subsided into somewhat shamefaced silence. If Muhammad had indeed meant to name an heir, he had left it too late. He no longer had the strength to make his final wishes known, let alone to quiet down the argument. Perhaps he was not as lucid as he appeared, or perhaps everyone in the room truly did have his best interests at heart, or the community's, but it is no contradiction to say that more was involved. Nearly every person there surely feared that Muhammad was about to put in writing what he had indicated just three months before, at the end of his last pilgrimage to Mecca—or as it would soon be called, the Final Pilgrimage.

Had he sensed then that he would never see Mecca again? That he didn't have much longer to live? Was that why he had made such a point of singling out Ali the way he did?

Shia scholars would maintain that he had a clear intimation of mortality, and that he prefaced his declaration with these words: "The time approaches when I shall be called away by God and I shall answer that call. I am leaving you with two precious things and if you adhere to both of them, you will never go astray. They are the Quran, the Book of God, and my family, the People of the House, *Ahl al-Bayt*. The two shall never separate from each other until they come to me by the pool of Paradise."

Sunni scholars dispute this. These words were added later, they say, and besides, they do not indicate that Muhammad knew he was soon to die. Like anyone of sixty-three, when the human body makes its age known in ways a younger person never imagines, he certainly knew he would not live forever, but that did not mean he expected to die in the near future. He was merely preparing the assembled Muslims for the inevitable, whenever it would come.

The time and place of Muhammad's declaration are not in dispute. It was on March 10 in the year 632, three months before his final illness. The caravan of returning pilgrims had stopped for the night at the spring-fed water hole known as Ghadir Khumm, the Pool of Khumm. It was not the picturesque Hollywood image of an oasis, but oasis it was: a shallow pool with just enough moisture in the sand around it to nurture the undemanding roots of a few scraggly palm trees. In the barren mountains of western Arabia, even the smallest spring was a treasured landmark, and this one more than most since it was where several caravan routes intersected. Here the thousands of returning pilgrims would break up into smaller parties, some going on to Medina and other points north, others to the east. This was the last night they would all be together, and their numbers were swelled by the arrival of Ali at the head of a force returning from a mission to the Yemen. He had been successful: Yemenite opposition to Muhammad had been quelled, and taxes and tribute paid. Celebration was in the air. It was the perfect time, it seemed, for Muhammad to honor his former protégé, now a mature man of thirty-five, a warrior returning with mission accomplished.

That evening, after they had watered the camels and horses, after they had cooked and eaten and chosen sleeping places under the palms, Muhammad ordered a raised platform made out of palm branches with camel saddles placed on top—a kind of makeshift desert pulpit—and at the end of the communal prayer he climbed on top of it. With that flair for the dramatic gesture for which he was famed, he called on Ali to climb onto the pulpit alongside him, reaching out his hand to help the younger man up. Then he raised Ali's hand high in his own, forearm pressed along forearm in the traditional gesture of allegiance, and in front of the thousands of people gathered below them, he honored the younger man with a special benediction.

"He of whom I am the master, of him Ali is also the master," he said. "God be the friend of he who is his friend, and the enemy of he who is his enemy."

It seemed clear enough at the time. Certainly Omar thought it was. He came up to Ali and congratulated him. "Now morning and evening you are the master of every believing man and woman," he said.

Surely this meant that Omar had taken Muhammad's declaration to mean that Ali was now formally his heir, and it is hard to imagine that Omar was the only one to understand Muhammad's words this way. But again, there is that fatal ambiguity. If Muhammad had indeed intended this as a formal designation, why had he not simply said so? Why rely on symbolism instead of a straightforward declaration? In fact, why had he not declared it during the *hajj,* in Mecca, when the greatest concentration of Muslims were all in one place? Was this just a spontaneous out-pouring of love and affection for his closest kinsman, or was it intended as more?

In the three months to come, as in the fourteen hundred years since, everything was up for interpretation, including what it was exactly that Muhammad had said. We know what words were used, but what did they mean? Arabic is a language of intricate subtleties. The word usually translated as "master" is *mawla*, which can mean leader, or patron, or friend and confidant. It all depends on context, and context is infinitely debatable. Omar could simply have been acknowledging what every Muslim, Shia and Sunni alike, still acknowledges, which is that Ali was a special friend to all Muslims.

Moreover, the second part of Muhammad's declaration at Ghadir Khumm was the standard formula for pledging allegiance or friendship throughout the Middle East of the time—"God be the friend of he who is your friend, the enemy of he who is your enemy"—the formula much degraded in modern political parlance into the misguidedly simplistic "The enemy of my enemy is my friend." But even in its original form, this did not necessarily imply inheritance. As a declaration of trust and confidence in Ali, it was accepted by all. But did that mean it was a declaration of Ali as the Prophet's successor?

The more things seemed to be clear, the less clear they had become.

What would Muhammad have written if the pen and paper had arrived? That Ali would be his *khalifa*, his successor, say the Shia. Who knows? say the Sunnis—a matter of no importance, blown out of all proportion by the overactive imaginations of the Shia faithful. After all, if there are any number of ways to interpret a written document, there are an infinite number of ways to interpret one that was never written at all.

There can be no resolution to such an argument. Everyone claimed to know the answer—everyone still does—but the early biographies and histories report what people did and what they said, not what they thought or intended. And the crux of the argument hinges not on what happened but on what it meant.

As always, the question is what Muhammad was thinking—a question that will be asked in turn about Ali too, and, after him, about his son Hussein. What did they intend? What did they know or not know? Unanswerable questions all, which is why the wrenching rift in Islam is so enduring. Despite all the impassioned claims, all the religious certainties and fiery oratory and ghastly massacres to come, the enduring irony is that "absolute" truth is the one thing that can never be established. It does not exist even in science; how much less so in history.

All we know for sure is that in the grip of fever, blinded by those agonizing headaches that made every sound seem as if it were piercing into his skull, Muhammad was no longer in any condition to impose his will. The pen and paper never arrived, and by dawn the next morning he was so weak he could barely move.

He knew then that the end was near because he made one last request, and this one was granted. He was to be washed with seven pails of water from seven different wells, he said, and though he did not explain it, all his wives were certainly aware that this was part of the ritual for washing a corpse. They washed him, and once he was in a state of ritual purity, he asked to be taken across the courtyard to morning prayers in the mosque.

It took two men, Ali and his uncle Abbas, to support him, one on either side of him, his arms around their necks. The few yards from Aisha's chamber to the mosque itself must have seemed an infinite distance, and the shade of the mosque an exquisite relief from the blinding sun. When they reached it, Muhammad gestured to be seated beside the pulpit, where he could watch as his old friend Abu Bakr led the prayers in his place.

Those who were there remembered the Prophet smiling as the voice of his loyal companion sounded through the building. They said his face was radiant, though there is no knowing if it was the radiance of faith or the radiance of fever and impending death. Perhaps it was the radiance of their own faith, of their gratitude at seeing him there. They watched as he sat and listened to the chanting of the words he had first heard from the angel Gabriel, and persuaded themselves that it was not the last time. But once the prayers were over and Ali and Abbas had carried him back to Aisha's chamber, Muhammad had only a few hours left.

Some were more clearsighted than others. "I swear by God that I saw death in the Prophet's face," Ali's uncle told him after they had settled the sick man back onto his pallet and left Aisha's chamber. Now was the last chance to clarify the matter of succession. "Let us go back and ask. If authority be with us, we shall know it, and if it be with others, we will ask him to direct them to treat us well."

But Ali would hear nothing of it. "By God I will not," he said. "If it is withheld from us, none after him will give it to us." Not even Ali, it seemed, was ready for too much clarity.

By then, in any case, it was too late. Even as the two men were talking, Muhammad lapsed into unconsciousness, and this time he did not recover. By noon of that Monday, June 8 in the year 632, he was dead.

He died, Aisha would say, with his head on her breast—or, as the original Arabic has it with vivid delicacy, "between my lungs and my lips." That is the Sunni version. But the Shia say that Muhammad's head lay not on Aisha's breast but on Ali's. It was Ali's arms that cradled the dying prophet in his last moments, they say, and Ali who heard the Prophet, with his dying breath, repeat his chilling last words three times: "Oh God, have pity on those who will succeed me."

Who held the dying prophet matters. Whose ears heard that final breath, whose skin it touched, whose arms supported him as he passed from life to death matter with particular intensity. It is as though his last breath had carried his spirit, leaping from his body at the precise moment of death to enter the soul of the one who held him. That was the person who held not only the past but the future of Islam in his arms. Or hers.

chapter 5

No words were needed to carry the news. The wailing did that. First Aisha, then all the other wives broke into a terrible, piercing howl that sounded for all the world like a wounded animal hiding in the bush to die. It spoke of ultimate agony, of pain and sorrow beyond all comprehension, and it spread through the oasis at the speed of sound.

Men and women, old and young, everyone took up the wail and surrendered themselves to it. They slapped their faces with both hands, a rapid rat-a-tat on either cheek; beat their chests with clenched fists so that the sound echoed as though the whole torso were a hollow tree; raked their foreheads with their fingernails until blood streaked down over their eyes and their tears were stained red; scooped up handfuls of dust from the ground and poured it over their heads, abasing themselves in despair. These were the time-honored rituals of grief, the same public rituals still carried out every year at Ashura, when the Shia mourn the tragic death of Ali's son Hussein. They were the outward expression of abandonment, of being abandoned and of abandoning oneself to mourning—not only for the one who had died but for themselves, leaderless, without him.

"We were like sheep on a rainy night," one of the Emigrants was to recall—moving this way and that in panic, with nobody to guide them and no shelter to be found. How could the Prophet be dead? Hadn't they just seen him in the mosque, his face radiant as they chanted the responses to prayer? It was so awful a thing to contemplate, so impossible to get one's mind around, that even Omar, the bravest of warriors, could not absorb it. The man who had asserted with such authority that the Book of God, the Quran, was sufficient, now refused to accept that death had won the day.

It could not be so, Omar insisted. It was heresy even to entertain such an idea. Muhammad was gone only for the moment. There would be a resurrection, as there had been with the last great prophet, Jesus. The Messenger would return from the dead and lead his people to the Day of Judgment. And in a panic of blind grief, before anyone could stop him, this most severe of men stood up in the forecourt of the mosque and berated the fearful crowd.

"By God, he is not dead," he declared, even as the tears ran down his face and over his beard. "He has gone to his lord as the prophet Moses went and was hidden from his people for forty days, returning to them after it was said that he had died. By God, the Messenger will return as Moses returned and will cut off the hands and feet of all men who allege that he is dead!"

But if this was intended to calm the wailing crowd, it had the opposite effect. The sight of Omar in hysterical denial only gave rise to greater panic. It took the small, elderly figure of Abu Bakr to pull Omar back. "Gently, gently," he said, "be quiet"—and one can almost hear it, the soothing tone, urging calmness as he took the towering warrior by the arm and slowly led him aside, then took his place before the terrified throng.

His voice was startlingly strong, not at all what one would expect from such a frail body, and though the message he delivered was a terrible one, it was also oddly reassuring. "For those who worshiped Muhammad, Muhammad is dead," he announced. "For those who worship God, God is alive, immortal." The Messenger is dead, long live Islam.

There was a sudden silence as Abu Bakr's words sank in, and then Omar's knees gave way and he collapsed to the ground, bent over in agonized tears. The older man's calm realism had subdued the terrifying giant, turned him into a weeping child, and as Abu Bakr continued, reciting the revelation that was to become part of Sura 3 of the Quran, everyone wept along with Omar.

"Muhammad is naught but a Messenger," Abu Bakr declaimed. "Messengers have passed away before him. Why, if he should die or be slain, should you turn back on your heels?"

And with this confirmation of mortality, as the tears flowed and the agonized wailing continued through the day and far into the night so that even the pack animals were restless in their pens and the jackals and hyenas in the mountains all around Medina could be heard raising their voices in unison, reality began to set in.

For some, however, it was to set in faster than for others.

Ali and three of his kinsmen had shut themselves in Aisha's chamber and begun the work of the closest male relatives, preparing Muhammad for the grave. Theirs was the long, slow ritual task of washing him and rubbing herbs over him and wrapping him in his shroud. But even in grief, others were thinking of the future. The "lost sheep" were faced with the daunting task of selecting one of their own as their shepherd.

Within the hour, the lingering distrust between the native Medinans and the former Meccans had surfaced. Ibn Obada, the head of one of Medina's two main tribes, put out the call for a *shura,* a traditional intertribal forum where agreements were ratified and disputes settled. It was a kind of seventh-century version of the smoke-filled back room, and like that back room, it was strictly by invitation only. The call went out quickly, but only among the native Medinans, the ones known as the Helpers. The Meccans, those known as the Emigrants, were not invited.

The Medinan Helpers had trusted Muhammad because they considered him a kinsman. Since his father's mother had been born in Medina, they had seen him as one of their own. But the seventy-two companions who had followed him from Mecca, along with their families, were another matter. They had been welcomed, of course, but not with the most open of arms. True, all were equal in Islam. All were brothers, all family. But even between brothers—or perhaps especially between brothers—resentment and ill will flourished. The Emigrants remained Meccans in the eyes of the Helpers, tolerated in Medina rather than accepted. They were still members of that rival city's ruling Quraysh tribe, and now, in the sudden absence of Muhammad as the unifying force, the politics of tribe and clan would reassert themselves.

The *shura* took time, for its success depended on consensus. That was a high ideal, but in practice it meant that the session would go on until those opposed to the general feeling of the meeting had been persuaded or worn down or simply browbeaten into going along with the majority. Such things could not be hurried. Each leader, each elder, each representative had to have his say, and at length.

Few there could read or write, but their powers of oratory were phenomenal, as was often the way in preliterate societies. Ornate rhetoric was not merely valued; its display was a pleasure in its own right. The poetry of a speech was as important as its content, its length a measure of the speaker's worth and standing, and this now acted against the interests of the Medinans. A meeting of this importance could not be kept secret for long. Word got out, and just a few hours after the *shura* had begun, those not invited—the Meccan Emigrants—decided to invite themselves.

By early evening of that fateful Monday, Abu Bakr had roused Omar from his grief. There would be time enough to mourn once the succession to Muhammad had been settled, he said. The Medinans could not be allowed to break away; that would work against everything Muhammad had achieved. The new leader of Islam had to be someone who would unite, not divide, the Muslim community.

Like Abu Bakr, Omar had taken it for granted that this leader would be one of the Emigrants. They were the Prophet's earliest companions, the men who had been with him the longest, and the most influential of them were three senior counselors besides Ali: Omar himself, Abu Bakr, and a third man—Othman, the handsome aristocrat from the Umayyads, the wealthiest clan of Mecca's Quraysh tribe.

While most of the Umayyads had opposed Muhammad until just two years before, Othman had accepted Islam early on. He had emigrated to Medina with the Prophet, given most of his wealth to the cause, and steadfastly supported it even when it meant battle against his own kin. In gratitude, Muhammad had honored him with the hand of his second daughter in marriage and then, when she died, with that of his third. Othman thus had the unique distinction of being the double son-in-law of the Prophet. His voice would be essential if Omar and Abu Bakr were to prevail.

He had not been there in the sickroom in the final days of Muhammad's illness; as is the way of the aristocrat, he exercised the prerogative of wealth and spent most of the midsummer months in his mountain estate outside Medina, where the air was fresher and cooler. But his presence was vital now, and word was sent to him posthaste. With or without invitation, the Emigrants were going to the *shura,* and Othman should join them there as quickly as he could.

Led by Omar and Abu Bakr, they turned up in force and muscled their way in. Essentially, they gate-crashed the meeting, outnumbering those already there. Only one person with a direct interest in the proceedings would remain absent, but for many, that absence would deprive the *shura* of all legitimacy.

Ali was the one Emigrant whom the native Medinans would have freely acknowledged as their leader. They saw him more as one of theirs than as a Meccan. Since Muhammad was their kin because of his grand-mother, so too was Ali, Muhammad's closest male relative. Yet it was precisely because he was the closest male relative that Ali would remain absent.

He must certainly have heard about the *shura*. His uncle Abbas—the same uncle who had pleaded with him just that morning to go back to Muhammad and clarify the succession—surely urged him to leave his vigil over the Prophet's body, and offered to keep watch in his place. With so much at stake, it was vital that Ali assert his right to leadership.

If Abbas made the argument, though, he made it in vain. One can see Ali shaking his head—in sorrow? in disgust?—not at the idea of the *shura* but at its being held with such unseemly haste. Before the Prophet had even been buried? To leave the man who had been father and mentor to him before consigning him back to the earth from which he had come? However dire the circumstances, that was out of the question. Ali was above all a man of faith; he would stay with the body, in the faith that the Medinans would support him.

It would not be the last time he would suffer from misplaced faith in others.

To Sunnis, the *shura* would be the perfect example of the wisdom of consensus, of a community newly empowered to resolve its disputes and to find the right solution. The Prophet trusted them to find the right leader, they maintained. In fact that was precisely what he had intended all along. They would quote a later tradition in which Muhammad said, "My community will never agree in error." The Islamic community was sacred, that is, and thus by definition free of error. But in centuries to come, this statement came to serve as a self-fulfilling argument against the Shia. It would be taken to mean that any Muslims who disagreed with the Sunni majority could only be in error; the Shia, by force of their disagreement, were not part of the true community of Islam as defined by Sunnis.

For the Shia, it was not the community but the leadership that was sacred. The Sunnis had abrogated divinely ordained power by determining it among themselves, they would argue, and this usurpation of the divine had begun right there, in the first Islamic *shura*. The Prophet's will had been clear: Ali was the only true, legitimate successor to the Prophet. To acclaim anyone else as Caliph was a betrayal not only of Muhammad but of Islam itself.

It seems clear that the *shura* began with the best intentions, but even as unity was the one thing people most wanted, it was also the one thing that seemed impossible to achieve. The moment the crowd of Meccan Emigrants burst in, the Medinan Helpers knew that their bid to claim leadership for one of their own was doomed. In an attempt at compromise, they proposed separate leaders. "Let us Helpers have one rule and you Emigrants another," they said. But Abu Bakr and Omar insisted on one leader for the whole of Islam, and that leader, they argued, had to be an Emigrant. They had been the earliest to accept Islam. They were from Muhammad's own tribe, the Quraysh, who had transformed Mecca into a great trading and pilgrimage center. Islam was about unity, they said, and only someone from the Quraysh could keep Mecca and Medina together as one people, the center of the community of Islam.

Inevitably, the *shura* dragged on, through the night and into the next day. Speech followed speech—long, ornate, impassioned orations. All had the welfare of the people in mind, as such speeches always do. There is no doubting the public concern of all those involved, nor the self-interest. Public concern and self-interest do sometimes coincide, even—especially—when the self-interest is your own.

The Emigrants began to impose their will on the Helpers. It became clear that the successor would be Quraysh, from Mecca. That much was now certain, but which one? All else being equal, the established principle of *nasb*, noble lineage, might have held sway. This held that nobility was in the bloodline, and in a society so entranced by lineage that later, when outright civil war had begun, warriors would stand tall and proclaim their lineage aloud before actually attacking each other, bloodlines mattered. By the principle of *nasb,* Ali should have been the successor.

But all else was not equal. Despite Muhammad's personal authority, his clan—and Ali's—was relatively powerless within the large Quraysh tribe. They were Hashimis, and the Quraysh were dominated by the Umayyads, who had led the opposition to Muhammad for so many years, their wealth and power threatened by his preaching of equality.

The Hashimis had been honored by having the Prophet come from their clan, the argument now went. But now that he was gone, the honor of leadership had to be extended to other clans of the Quraysh. Muhammad's intention had always been to spread power wide, not to raise up one clan above all others. To choose Ali, another Hashimi, would be to risk turning the leadership of Islam into a form of hereditary monarchy, and that was the opposite of everything Muhammad had stood for. Leadership was not something to be inherited, like property. It had to be decided by merit, not by blood. This was what Muhammad had intended all along. This was why he had never formally declared an heir. He had faith in the people's ability to decide for themselves, in the sanctity of the decision of the whole community.

It was an argument for democracy, in however limited a form—an argument against exactly what would happen just fifty years into the future, when an Umayyad Caliph in Damascus would establish a Sunni dynasty by handing over his throne to his son, with disastrous consequences for Ali's son Hussein. It was in fact an argument against all the dynasties to come over the ensuing centuries, whether caliphates, shahdoms, sultanates, principalities, kingdoms, or presidencies. But it was also an argument for returning power to those who were used to the exercise of it, the Umayyads.

Whether in the seventh century or the twenty-first, the East or the

West, the habit of power is ingrained in certain families and clans. It is an attitude, a built-in assumption of one's right to rule, to carry on what in democracies is called "a tradition of public service," and it is passed on from one generation to the next even without the institution of hereditary kingship. It was this attitude that distinguished the Quraysh as a whole, and, among them, the Umayyads in particular. So if there was one possible candidate at the *shura* who seemed to have been born to power, it was Othman, the Umayyad. But not in this city. Until Mecca had submitted to Islam two years before, Meccan armies led by Umayyads had fought two major battles against Muhammad and Medina, not to mention countless skirmishes. With the memory of those battles still fresh in their minds and the scars still livid on their flesh, none of the Medinan Helpers would agree to an Umayyad as their leader, even one as respected as Othman.

As the light faded on the Tuesday evening, the *shura* seemed to have reached deadlock. Most of those present were near the point of exhaustion. They had sat through more than twenty-four hours of speeches, proposals, and counterproposals, yet consensus seemed further away than ever. Then, with what might be seen as the finesse of an endgame in a champion chess match, Abu Bakr and Omar made their closing move.

Had they worked it out beforehand? Nobody would ever know, but it went so smoothly, with such an air of inevitability, that Ali's followers would always suspect that it had been planned all along.

First, Abu Bakr proposed Omar as the new leader of Islam, though he must have known that after Omar's panic-stricken speech denying Muhammad's death, the tall warrior was not exactly the man of the moment. Then Omar responded by proposing that Othman be the leader, though he in turn must have known that since Othman was Umayyad, this was a nonstarter. Sure enough, both proposals provoked heated opposition, and tempers finally frayed beyond the breaking point.

Speeches gave way to shouting, outward calm to heated finger-pointing. Ibn Obada, the Medinan Helper who had originally convened the *shura*, stood up and openly accused the Emigrants of working in collusion to take over the leadership. No sooner were the words out of his mouth than several of the Emigrants leaped on him, fists flying. In the ensuing free-for-all, he was beaten unconscious.

The sudden outburst of violence seemed to sap the resistance of the Medinans. They were dismayed at seeing Ibn Obada carried out with his head bloodied, and in shock that a *shura* should come to this. All desire for any further debate seeped out of them, so that when the final proposal came, they simply gave in. In a move that the Shia have ever since claimed was rigged beforehand, and that Sunnis acclaim as the perfect example of the wisdom of consensus, Omar suddenly came up with what he presented as the ideal compromise.

His account of it has all the terse brevity of a military man: "Altercation waxed hotter and voices were raised until, when a complete breach was to be feared, I said 'Stretch out your hand, Abu Bakr.'

"He did so and I pledged him allegiance. The Emigrants followed, and then the Helpers."

And so it was done. The successor to Muhammad—the *khalifa*, the Caliph—was not Ali. It was the father of Muhammad's most prominent widow, the ever-controversial Aisha.

The burial would be strangely hugger-mugger. It was done in haste—indeed, in secrecy—and with a matter-of-factness that seems startling in the light of all the pilgrimages and sacred precincts to come.

By the time Ali and his kinsmen heard the news of Abu Bakr's election, Muhammad had been dead a full day and a half, and for reasons all too obvious in the intense June heat, the matter of burial was becoming urgent. Custom decreed that a body be buried within twenty-four hours, but with all the tribal and clan leaders at the *shura*, there had seemed no option but to wait. Now that the *shura* had agreed on a leader, however, Abu Bakr was likely to make Muhammad's funeral a major occasion, a stage for confirmation of his election, and this was exactly what Ali would deny him. There would be no funeral, just burial in the dead of night.

In the small hours of that Wednesday morning, Aisha was woken by scraping sounds echoing around the mosque courtyard. While Muhammad's body lay in her chamber, she had moved in with her co-wife Hafsa, Omar's daughter, a few doors down. In the exhaustion of grief, however, she could not rouse herself to investigate the noise. If she had, she would have discovered that what had woken her was the sound of steel digging into rocky soil. With pickaxes and shovels, Ali and his kinsmen were digging Muhammad's grave, and they were digging it in Aisha's chamber.

Muhammad had once said that a prophet should be buried where he had died, they explained later. Since he had died on the sleeping platform in Aisha's chamber, that was where he had to be buried, so they dug the grave at the foot of the platform, and when it was deep enough, they tipped up the pallet holding the Prophet's shrouded body, slid it down into the earth, quickly covered it, and placed the stone slab of the platform on top.

None of the wives was present, nor any of the other Emigrants, nor any of the Helpers. It was a fait accompli, as final in its way as the decision of the *shura*. Aisha's chamber, the place she had lived and eaten and slept, was now the grave of the Prophet, and her father was the new leader of Islam, the first of three Caliphs over the next twenty-five years—none of them Ali. What he was to call his "years of dust and thorns" were about to begin.

Part Two

Ali

chapter 6

IF YOU WERE A BELIEVER IN FATE, YOU MIGHT THINK THAT ALI was destined never to be Caliph, and that when he finally did accept the caliphate twenty-five years after Muhammad's death, he was provoking fate and thus the tragedy that would follow. He would be passed over not once or even twice, but three times in those twenty-five years, and all that time, he said, he lived "with dust in my eyes and thorns in my mouth."

Dust and thorns are a vivid image of life in exile—not physical but existential exile, from one's sense of purpose and self. But for Ali, the image was also cruelly ironic. The Lion of God was only one of the many titles the Prophet had bestowed on him; the one that would haunt him now was *Abu Turab*, Father of Dust. A lowly title to Western ears, but not to Arabian ones.

Some say that the name came from the dust thrown up by the hooves of Ali's horse as he charged into battle. Others that it was from the time Muhammad found his young cousin deep in meditative prayer despite a raging sandstorm, his robe white with blown dust. Yet others that it came from the early years in Medina, when Ali had worked as a manual laborer, hauling stones and water, an image that was to establish him as the champion of working people, a bridge between the early Arabian Muslims and the new Muslim masses to come.

All three are possible, and in all, the dust was a mark of honor. It still is. The Shia faithful still gather dust from the sandy soil of Najaf, the city surrounding Ali's gold-domed shrine a hundred miles south of Baghdad, then press it into small clay tablets that they place in front of them as they pray so that wherever in the world a Shia prostrates himself in prayer, the soil his forehead touches is sacred soil.

That same soil is where Shia from all over the Middle East still ask to be sent for burial, as they have for hundreds of years. The shrouded bodies once transported like rolled-up carpets by mule and camel now arrive by car and truck. They are carried in procession around the shrine of Ali in Najaf or that of his son Hussein in Karbala, then to one of the vast twin cemeteries known as the Vales of Peace, there to rise together with Ali and Hussein on the Day of Judgment, when their descendant the Mahdi will return to lead a new era of truth and justice.

But truth and justice must have seemed a long way off to Ali in those days after Muhammad's death. "Woe to the Helpers of the Prophet and to his kin," wrote one of his Medinan supporters. "The land has become narrow for the Helpers and their faces have turned black as *kohl*. We have given birth to the Prophet and among us is his tomb. Would that on that day they covered him in his grave and cast soil on him, God had left not a single one of us, and neither man nor woman had survived him. We have been humiliated."

A Hashimi poet put it more succinctly: "We have been cheated in the most monstrous way."

They had been disinherited, deprived of what they saw as their rightful place, the leadership of Islam. And this sense of disinheritance would sear deep into Shia hearts and minds, a wound that would fester through to the twentieth century, there to feed off opposition to Western colonialism and erupt first in the Iranian Revolution, then in civil war in Lebanon, and then, as the twenty-first century began, in the war in Iraq. Disinheritance was a rallying cry, which was why the classic anticolonial text of the 1960s, Frantz Fanon's *The Wretched of the Earth*, became an Iranian best seller with a pointed change in title, one specifically designed to speak to the Shia experience: *The Disinherited of the Earth*. The time was coming, as it eventually would for Ali himself, when the Shia would reclaim their inheritance, in however embattled a form. But first, the dust and thorns.

The thorns were felt immediately. Even while others lined up to pledge public allegiance to Abu Bakr as Caliph, the man who had been passed over remained with his family inside his house. He was in mourning, he declared, and this was certainly so, but his refusal to come out and pledge allegiance to Abu Bakr was also a clear gesture of defiance, and a major challenge. If Ali held out, the Medinan Helpers might renege on their allegiance and follow him, overturning the outcome of the *shura*. Ali had to be pulled into line, and quickly, so Abu Bakr delegated Omar to deal with the problem. But by doing so, he only worsened it.

The choice of a stern military man like Omar for what was surely a diplomatic task was at the least unfortunate. Omar's courage and skill as a commander were beyond question, but so too was his reputation as a man quick with the whip, "too severe" to bother with verbal niceties. He was not a man of finesse, and he demonstrated as much that night. He gathered a group of armed men, led them to Ali's house, stationed them around it, then planted himself right in front of the door. Ali should come out and pledge allegiance to Abu Bakr, he shouted. If not, he and his men would burn down the house.

"If I had had only forty men, I would have resisted with force," Ali said later. But that night only the members of his immediate family were with him: the *Ahl al-Bayt*, the People of the House. Ali chose passive resistance instead, and refused to budge.

Short of actually following through on his threat and killing all of Muhammad's closest family, Omar was left, as he saw it, with only one option. If Ali would not come out, then he, Omar, would have to force his way in. He took a running leap and threw his whole weight against the door, and when the latches and hinges gave and it burst open, all six feet of him came hurtling through, unable to stop as he slammed full force into the person who happened to be on the other side of the door at that moment. That person was Fatima, several months pregnant with the Prophet's third grandson.

Some say she was only badly bruised. Others that she broke her arm as she fell. But all agree that even Omar was stunned by the sight of the Prophet's heavily pregnant daughter doubled over in pain at his feet. As Ali bent over his injured wife, Omar retreated without another word. He had made his point.

A few weeks later, the fragile Fatima gave birth to a stillborn infant boy. Nobody was sure if the miscarriage was a result of her being knocked down by Omar or whether she was so frail that it would have happened regardless. Either way, some overture might have been warranted from Abu Bakr, or at least from Omar, but there was none. Indeed, there was less than none.

To add insult to the injury that had already been done her, Fatima would now lose the property she considered hers. Soon after her miscarriage, she sent a message to Abu Bakr asking for her share of her father's estate—date palm orchards in the huge oases of Khaybar and Fadak to the north of Medina. His response left her dumbfounded. The Prophet's estate belonged to the community, not to any individual, Abu Bakr replied. It was part of the Muslim charitable trust, to be administered by him as Caliph. He was not at liberty to give it away to individuals. "We do not have heirs," he said Muhammad had told him. "Whatever we leave is alms."

Fatima had no alternative but to accept his word for it. Abu Bakr's reputation for probity was beyond question, whatever her suspicions.

Sunnis would later hail his stand as affirming the supremacy of the community over individual hereditary rights. "You are not the People of the House," Abu Bakr seemed to be saying. "We are all the People of the House." But the Shia would be convinced that Muhammad's closest family had now been doubly disinherited, or cheated, as the poet would have it: Ali out of his inheritance of leadership, and Fatima out of her inheritance of property.

There was no denying the populist appeal of the message Abu Bakr sent by denying Fatima's claim: the House of Muhammad was the House of Islam, and all were equal within it. But as ever, some were more equal than others. Even as he turned down Fatima, Abu Bakr made a point of providing generously for Muhammad's widows—and particularly for his own daughter Aisha, who received valuable property in Medina as well as on the other side of the Arabian Peninsula, in Bahrain.

It was the final straw for Fatima. That her father's uppity youngest wife should be rewarded and she, his firstborn by his first and most beloved wife, should be rebuffed? She never did recover from her miscarriage or from the bitter argument with Abu Bakr. But perhaps most painful of all in those months after the loss of her third son was the ostracism she suffered, ordered by Abu Bakr to force Ali into line.

In a close-knit society, boycott is a powerful weapon. The pressure to conform mounts as day by day, week by week, you become increasingly invisible. People turn their backs; friends keep their distance; acquaintances pass by in silence, staring through you as though you were not there. Even in the mosque, Ali prayed alone.

Ironically, the same weapon had earlier been used in Mecca against Muhammad and his clan. Despite its power, it had failed then, which was why the Meccan elite had resorted to attempted murder, and it would fail now. Fatima refused to bow to the pressure. When she knew death was close, she asked Ali for a clandestine burial like that of her father less than three months before. Abu Bakr was not to be informed of her death, she said; he was to be given no chance to officiate at her funeral.

She was to be buried quietly, with only her close family, the true *Ahl al-Bayt*, in attendance.

If Aisha felt any sense of triumph on hearing of her rival's death, she was unusually quiet about it. But she had no need to exult. She was now doubly honored: the widow of the Prophet and the daughter of his successor. Triply honored, indeed, for her chamber by the courtyard wall of the mosque was also Muhammad's grave.

You can see how some might treasure the image of the young widow sleeping with her husband buried under her bed. It has a touch of magical realism, like a scene from a novel by Gabriel García Márquez, but this is no novel, and the reality is that Aisha never slept in her chamber again. All the widows were moved out into private quarters away from the mosque, each with a generous pension—and Aisha's more generous than the others. She would not eat and sleep for the rest of her life in the company of her dead husband, though she would certainly live as if she did.

Where she had striven so hard to own Muhammad in life, it now seemed she would succeed in owning him in death. She would become a major source of *hadith*—the reports on the Prophet's practice, or *sunna*, in things large and small, from great matters of principle to the most minute details of when he washed and how, even what kind of toothpick he used to clean his teeth. The Sunnis would eventually name themselves for the *sunna*; they would own it, as it were, despite the fact that the Shia honor it too.

Yet no matter how many *hadith* would be attributed to Aisha—and there were thousands—the future would not be kind to her. As long as she lived, she was honored as the leading Mother of the Faithful, but in memory she was destined to remain an embattled symbol of slandered virtue. In later centuries, conservative clerics would point to her as an example of the division they claimed ensues when women enter public life, as Aisha would so disastrously when Ali finally became Caliph. Everything that makes her so interesting to the secular mind—her ambition, her outspokenness, her assertiveness—would work against her in the Islamic mind, even among Sunnis.

And no matter how pale an image Fatima left in comparison with Aisha, no matter that she died young and never got a chance to dictate her own version of history, time would favor her. The Shia would call her Al-Zahra, the Radiant One. If she seemed anything but radiant in life—a pale, almost self-effacing presence—that was of no importance. This was radiance of spirit, the pure light of holiness, for the Prophet's bloodline ran through Fatima and into her two sons.

In Shia lore, Fatima lives on in another dimension to witness her sons' suffering and to weep for them. She is the Holy Mother, whose younger son would sacrifice himself to redeem humanity just as had the son of that other great mother, Mary. Like her, Fatima is often called the Virgin as a sign of her spiritual purity. Like her, she will mourn her offspring until the Day of Judgment, when legend has it that she will reappear, carrying the poisoned heart of Hasan in one hand and the severed head of Hussein in the other.

Ali honored Fatima's wishes. He buried her in the dead of night, as he had so recently buried her father, and then, after he had consigned her to the earth, he did what he had refused to do since he had been passed over as Caliph: He conceded, and pledged allegiance to Abu Bakr. Many said he acted in grief or even in despair, but in fact there were pressing reasons for him to do as he did.

As the news of Muhammad's death had spread throughout Arabia, rebellion had spread with it. Many of the tribes in the north and center of the vast peninsula threatened to break away from Islam, or at least from its taxes. This was not a matter of faith, they said, but of tribal autonomy. To pay tribute to the Prophet was one thing; to enrich the coffers of the Quraysh tribe was quite another.

As Muhammad had wished, Ali had been loyal to Fatima to the end, but there was now, he said, a higher call on his loyalty. This was no time to hold grudges. He would pledge allegiance to Abu Bakr for the sake of unity in the face of rebellion, for the good of the community, and to present a solid front against the forces of divisiveness. If this was a declaration of idealism over experience, so be it. Indeed, his followers later praised it as an act of utmost nobility, but then Ali would rarely be anything but noble. His highest virtue, it would also prove to be his greatest liability.

With Ali at last in support, Abu Bakr took a hard line with the rebel tribes. "If they withhold only a hobbling cord of what they gave the Prophet, I will fight them for it," he declared, and his choice of language was a deliberate insult. These were mere camel herders, he was saying, "boorish Beduin" in the eyes of the urbanized Quraysh aristocracy. The thousands of Arabic odes extolling the purity of desert life were no more than nostalgic idylls, much as pastoral images of shepherds and shepherdesses would later be in Europe, or the John Wayne cowboy in the United States. Actual shepherds and camel herders were something else. Indeed, the few Beduin who have not been absorbed into urban life are still scorned within the Arab world.

Abu Bakr declared that since the taxes belonged to Islam, to refuse them was an act of apostasy. And where grace could be extended to a nonbeliever, none could be offered an apostate, someone who had first accepted and then turned against the faith. Such a person was no longer protected by the Quranic ban on Muslims shedding the blood of Muslims. That was *haram*, taboo, in Islam. But since an apostate was to be considered an active enemy of Islam, to shed his blood was no longer taboo. It was now *halal*—permitted under Islamic law.

This was to become a familiar argument, one made over time by

Sunnis against Shia, by Shia against Sunnis, by extremists against moderates, by legalist clerics against Sufi mystics, and most notoriously perhaps, at least in the West, by the Ayatollah Khomeini against novelist Salman Rushdie. Declare your opponent an apostate, and as the Arabic phrasing goes, "his blood is *halal*."

The Wars of Apostasy—the *ridda* wars—were as ruthless as Abu Bakr had promised. Within the year, all resistance had been crushed, and within another, Muslim forces had begun to strike north out of Arabia. It seemed that under Abu Bakr, the first of the four Caliphs the Sunnis would call *rashidun*, "the rightly guided ones," Islam was poised to achieve its full potential. Yet a year later, even as his forces prepared to lay siege to the Byzantine-controlled city of Damascus far to the north, Abu Bakr lay deathly ill, struck by fever. He would be the only Islamic leader to die of natural causes for close on fifty years. This time, however, there would be no doubt about who was to be the successor.

Some Sunnis would later say that Abu Bakr acted as he did to spare the community the divisiveness it had gone through before his own election; others, that as the Arab conquest began, he wanted a strong military figure in command. The Shia would see it very differently, arguing that he was driven by his antagonism toward Ali and his desire to keep the younger man out of power. Whichever it may have been, Abu Bakr's deathbed declaration was clear: there would be no *shura,* no conclave of tribal chiefs and elders. Though he had been elected by consensus himself, Abu Bakr had good reason to distrust the process.

How then to proceed? In the days before Islam, it would have been simple enough; one of Abu Bakr's sons would have inherited his rule. Hereditary monarchy lasted so long through history because it established a clear line of succession, avoiding the messy business of negotiation, the political maneuvering, the difficult, wearing process of the fragile thing we now know as democracy. But Islam was essentially egalitarian. As Abu Bakr himself had argued when he prevailed over the proponents of Ali, leadership, like prophecy, was not to be inherited. He was thus faced with the questions that still dog even the best intentions in the Middle East: How does one impose democracy? How can it work when there is no prior acceptance of the process, when there is no framework already in place?

You might say that Abu Bakr settled on a middle course. He would appoint his successor, but appoint him on the basis of merit, not kinship. He would choose the man he saw as best suited to the task, and if that was the same man he had proposed at the *shura* just two years before, then this merely demonstrated how right he had been. In a move destined to be seen by the Shia as further evidence of collusion, the dying Abu Bakr appointed Omar the second Caliph.

Again, Ali had been outmaneuvered. Again, he had been passed over, and this time in favor of the man who had injured his wife and threatened to burn down his house. Yet even as Abu Bakr was buried alongside the Prophet—the second body to lie under what had once been Aisha's bed—Ali insisted that his supporters keep their peace. Instead of challenging Omar, he took the high road a second time. He had sworn allegiance to Abu Bakr and been a man of his word, and now that same word applied to Abu Bakr's appointed successor, no matter the history between them. And if anyone doubted his absolute commitment to Islamic unity, he laid such doubts to rest with a remarkable move. As Omar's rule began, Ali married Abu Bakr's youngest widow, Asma.

To the modern mind, marrying a former rival's widow might seem an act of revenge. In seventh-century Arabia, it was quite the opposite: a major gesture of reconciliation. Ali's marriage to Asma was a way of reaching out, of healing old divisions and transforming them into alliance, and with Ali, the healing impulse went deep: He formally adopted Asma's three-year-old son by Abu Bakr and, by so doing, extended a hand in another direction—to the boy's influential half sister Aisha.

Once again, though, Aisha remained unusually silent. If she felt that Ali had stolen part of her family, there is no record of it, though over the years, as her half brother grew to manhood in Ali's house, her resentment of his loyalty to Ali would become all too clear, and the young man who should have bound the two antagonists together would only split them farther apart. For the meantime, however, that division would merely simmer, upstaged by a second even more remarkable union. In the strongest possible sign of unity, Ali honored the Caliph Omar by giving him the hand of his daughter Umm Kulthum—Muhammad's eldest granddaughter—in marriage.

The vast vine of marital alliance now reached across generations as well as political differences. Omar was the same generation as Muhammad yet had married his granddaughter. Ali, thirteen years younger than Omar, was now his father-in-law. And if Fatima turned in her modest grave at the idea of any daughter of hers being married to the man who had burst into her house and slammed her to the floor, that was the price of unity—that, and Omar's settlement of a large part of Muhammad's estates on Ali, exactly as Fatima had wanted.

Omar had now doubled his kinship to the Prophet: both father-in-law and grandson-in-law. His position as Caliph was secure. Ali could still have been a powerful rival, but Omar followed the ancient political dictum of keeping your friends close and your enemies closer. As son-in-law and father-in-law, the two men would work well together, so much so that every time Omar left Medina on one of his many military campaigns, Ali stood in as his deputy. It was a clear sign, understood by all to mean that when the time came, Ali would succeed Omar as Caliph.

The Arab conquest now began in earnest. Omar had taken Abu Bakr's title of Deputy to Muhammad but added another one: Commander of the Faithful. And a superb commander he was. He lived rough and ready with his troops on campaign, sleeping wrapped in his cloak on the desert floor and leading his men into battle instead of ordering them from the rear, thus earning their absolute loyalty and respect. If he had a reputation for strictness and discipline, it was balanced by his insistence on justice. As part of his commitment to Islam, he would tolerate no favoritism, least of all for his own family. When one of his own sons appeared drunk in public, Omar ordered that the young man be given eighty lashes of the whip, and refused to mourn when he died as a result of the punishment.

In the ten years of Omar's rule, the Muslims took control of the whole of Syria and Iraq, an expansion so rapid that it is still often explained by "a tribal imperative to conquest." The phrase is unknown to anthropologists, but it calls up an image of bloodthirsty peoples impelled by primitive urges, threatening the sane rationalism of the more civilized—the image incessantly echoed in current coverage of conflict in the Middle East.

In fact there was less blood involved than money. The Muslim forces did indeed win stunning military victories over the Persians and the Byzantines, despite being vastly outnumbered, but for the most part, the Arab conquest took place more by messenger than by the sword. Given the choice to accept Arab rule—albeit with the sword held in reserve—most of Islam's new subjects raised little objection. The Arabs, after all, were no strangers.

Long before Muhammad's ascent to power, Meccan aristocrats had owned estates in Egypt, mansions in Damascus, farms in Palestine, date orchards in Iraq. They had put down roots in the lands and cities they traded with, for to be a trader in the seventh century was to be a traveler, and to be a traveler was to be a sojourner. The twice-yearly Meccan caravans to Damascus—up to four thousand camels at a time—did not merely stop and go at that great oasis city. They stayed for months at a time while contacts were made, negotiations carried out, hospitality extended and provided. Arabian traders had long been part and parcel of the social, cultural, and economic life of the lands they were to conquer.

And the timing was perfect. Just as Islam had come into being, a vast vacuum of power had been created. The two great empires that had controlled the Middle East—the Byzantines to the west and the Persians to the east—were fading fast, having worn each other out with constant warfare. The Persians could no longer even afford the upkeep on the vast irrigation systems fed by the Tigris and Euphrates rivers in Iraq. The Byzantines' hold on Damascus and Jerusalem was tenuous at best. Both empires were collapsing from within, their power waning just as the Muslim nation was born, opening its eyes to what was practically an open invitation to enter and take over.

There was no imposition of Islam. On the contrary, Omar discouraged conversion. He wanted to keep Islam pure—that is, Arab—an attitude that would earn him no love among the Persians, who felt especially demeaned by it and would convert in large numbers after his death. He even ordered two new garrison cities built in Iraq—Basra in the south and Kufa in the center—to protect his administrators and troops from what he saw as Persian decadence.

But there was another strong incentive to keep conversion to a minimum. Omar had set up the *diwan*, a system by which every Muslim received an annual stipend, much as citizens of the oil-rich Gulf state of Dubai do today. It followed that the fewer Muslims there were, the larger the stipends, and since the taxes that provided these stipends were no greater than those previously paid to the Byzantines and the Persians, there was at first little resistance to them. As in any change of regime today, when photographs of the old ruler suddenly come down off the walls and ones of the new ruler go up, most people made their accommodations with Arab rule. But not everyone.

Nobody could have foreseen the assassination, the Medinans would say. It seemed to come out of the blue. How was anyone to know that a Christian slave from Persia would lose his mind and do such a dastardly thing? To stab the Caliph six times as he bent down for morning prayer in the mosque, then drive the dagger deep into his own chest? It was incomprehensible.

There would be hints of a conspiracy—veiled derision of the very idea of a lone gunman, as it were, instead of a sophisticated plot by dark forces intent on undermining the new Islamic empire. Yet in the seventh century, as in the twenty-first, people could be driven to irrational despair. Or in this case, perhaps, to rational desperation.

The story has it that the slave's owner had promised to free him but reneged on that promise. The slave had then appealed to Omar for justice, only to be rebuffed, and so bore an intense personal grudge against the Caliph. The story made sense, and people were glad to accept it. Even as Omar lay mortally wounded, even as they faced the death of their third leader in twelve years, there was nonetheless a palpable undercurrent of relief that the assassin was not one of theirs. He was Persian, not Arab; a Christian, not a Muslim. The assassination, terrible as it was, was the act of a madman, an outsider. Muslims did not kill Muslims. That was still *haram*, taboo—still the ultimate horror.

Again, the problem of succession faced a dying Caliph, and again, in the absence of an established process, the solution would be controversial, open to challenge for centuries to come. In the hours left before he died of his wounds, Omar decided on a middle course between the open consensus of a *shura* and the power to appoint his successor. As expected, he named Ali, but what nobody expected was that he also named five others—not one man, but six. These six, he decreed, were to be both the candidates and the electors. One of them would be his successor, but which one was up to them. They were to meet in closed caucus after his death and make their decision within three days.

Did he take it for granted that the electors would choose Ali? Surely that was so, yet two of the men he named were brothers-in-law of Aisha: her cousin Zubayr, as well as Talha, the man who had rashly declared his intention to marry her. And a third was Othman, the Umayyad aristocrat whom Abu Bakr had proposed as the leader of the *shura* after Muhammad's death. These were not people likely to agree to Ali as Caliph.

The moment Omar was buried—the third and final grave to be dug under Aisha's old sleeping platform—the six electors gathered in a room off the main part of the mosque. Omar had placed them in a terrible bind. If so much had not been at stake, it could almost be described as a fiendishly intricate game of strategy: six men trapped in a locked room, as it were, unable to leave until they cooperated even as cooperation was the last thing they were ready for. Each of the six wanted the leadership for himself, yet all six had to agree on which of them would get it. None wanted to be seen as wanting it too much, yet none was ready to concede.

By the third morning they had narrowed the choice to the two sons-in-law of the Prophet, Ali and Othman. To many outside that room, it seemed obvious which of the two should be Caliph. On the one hand was Ali, now in his mid-forties, the famed philosopher-warrior who had been the first man to accept Islam and who had served as deputy to both Muhammad and Omar. On the other was Othman, the pious and wealthy Umayyad who had converted early to Islam but had never actually fought in any battle and, at seventy, had already survived far beyond the average life span of the time. Nobody could have expected him to live much longer, and this would prove to be precisely his advantage.

If they settled on Othman over Ali, each of the others could buy time to position himself for the leadership the next time around. They saw Othman as a stopgap, a substitute until one or the other of them could muster enough support to take over when he died, surely a matter of no more than a year or two. Even as Ali could see the consensus building among the other men in the room, he was powerless to prevent it. As dusk fell on the third day, they preempted his assent by announcing their decision publicly in the mosque, and he knew then that his years of dust and thorns were not yet at an end. Left with no option, he pledged allegiance to yet another man as Caliph.

How bitter must it have been to see the leadership withheld from him yet again? How patient could he be? How noble in the name of unity? In the blinding light of hindsight, Ali should surely have been more assertive and insisted on his right to rule. But then he would not have been the man he was, the man famed for his nobility, his grace and integrity—a man too honorable, it seemed, for the rough-and-tumble of politics.

Or perhaps he too thought Othman would live only a short time.

chapter 7

IF OTHMAN HAD NOT BEEN BLESSED WITH GOOD GENES, MUCH blood might have gone unshed, including his own, so whether his longevity was indeed a blessing is a matter of some dispute. The fact remains that he defied all the odds and lived another twelve years, and when he died, at the age of eighty-two, it was not of old age. Like Omar before him, the third Caliph died under an assassin's knife. This time, however, the assassin was Muslim, and many would argue that he had excellent cause.

Othman was a man used to entitlement. He had been renowned for his good looks, as those who carry themselves with aristocratic ease and assurance often are. Despite his smallpox-scarred cheeks, people still talked admiringly of his "golden complexion" and his flashing smile—flashing not with whiteness but with the fine gold wire bound around his teeth as decoration. That emphasis on gold might perhaps have been a warning of what was to come.

His predecessor, Omar, had certainly foreseen it. When the spoils from the Persian court were sent to Medina, Omar had not smiled with satisfaction as all had hoped. Instead, he looked gravely at the piles of gold regalia, at the jewel-encrusted swords and the lavishly embroidered silks, and tears began to roll down his cheeks. "I weep," he'd said, "because riches beget enmity and mutual bitterness."

As the Arab empire expanded farther still under Othman—across Egypt to the west, all of Persia to the east, the Caspian Sea to the north—so too did its wealth, and with that wealth came exactly what Omar had feared. Muhammad had wrested control of Mecca from Othman's Umayyad clan, but with one of their own now in the leadership of Islam, the Umayyads seized the chance to reassert themselves as the aristocracy, men of title and entitlement, and Othman seemed unable—or unwilling—to resist them.

Nobody doubted his piety and devotion to Islam, but neither could anyone doubt his devotion to family. Top military positions, governorships, senior offices—all now went to Umayyads. Capable men were passed over for family cronies, and as might be expected when they had achieved their posts through nepotism, the new appointees were flagrantly corrupt. One senior general seethed in anger as his hard work went unrewarded and his authority was undermined by the greed of others. "Am I to hold the cow's horns while another man draws off the milk?" he protested.

Under Abu Bakr and Omar, Muhammad's ethic of simplicity and egalitarianism had prevailed, but now conspicuous consumption became the order of the day, exemplified in the extravagant new palace Othman had built in Medina, with enclosed gardens, marble columns, even imported food and chefs. Where both Abu Bakr and Omar had taken the relatively modest title of Deputy of Muhammad, Othman took a far more grandiose one. He insisted on being called the Deputy of God—the representative of God on earth—thus paving the way for the many future leaders all too eager to claim divine sanction for worldly power.

The old Meccan aristocracy rapidly became the new Muslim aristocracy. Othman began to deed vast private estates to his relatives, some with thousands of horses and as many slaves. In Iraq, so much of the rich agricultural land between the two rivers was given to Umayyad nobles that the whole of the Mesopotamian valley gained a new, ironic nickname, the Garden of the Umayyads. The other legacies of Othman's rule—the authoritative written compilation of the Quran and the further expansion of the empire north into the Aegean, west along the North African coast, and east to the frontiers of India—were increasingly overshadowed by what was seen as the Umayyad stranglehold on power.

The ruling class of Mecca was back in control, and with a vengeance. There was no doubt as to who was drawing the milk, and the ones left holding the horns became increasingly outspoken as nepotism and corruption devolved into their inevitable correlates: wrongful expropriation, deportation, imprisonment, even execution. The most respected early companions of Muhammad began to speak out in protest, as did all five of the other men who had sat in caucus and elected Othman, and none more clearly than Ali.

The property of Islam was being embezzled, he warned. The Umayyads were like a pack of hungry animals devouring everything in sight. "Othman shrugs his shoulders arrogantly, and his brothers stand with him, eating up the property of God as the camels eat up the springtime grasses." Once that brief treasured lushness was gone, only barren desert would be left.

But the voice that gained the most attention was that of Aisha, who found herself for once on the same side as Ali. "That dotard," she called Othman—a doddering old man in thrall to his relatives—and the word stuck, demeaning and mocking.

Some said she was roused to action only when Othman reduced her annual pension to that of the other Mothers of the Faithful, challenging her prominence. Others said she acted in the hope that her brother-in-law Talha would take over as Caliph. But there is also no doubt that Aisha was truly outraged by the extent of the corruption, which came to a head over the scandalous behavior of Walid, one of Othman's half brothers.

As the governor of the garrison city of Kufa in central Iraq, Walid did not even bother to disguise his aristocratic disdain for the residents under his control. With a kind of Arabian snobbery that would surface again and again, he contemptuously dismissed the native Iraqis as "provincial riffraff." Unjust imprisonment? Expropriation of lands? Embezzlement from the public treasury? Such complaints against him, Walid declared, were worth "no more than a goat's fart in the desert plains of Edom."

One particular goat's fart, however, would reach all the way to Medina when Walid appeared in the Kufa mosque flagrantly drunk and, in front of the assembled worshipers, vomited over the side of the pulpit. The Kufans sent a delegation to Medina to demand that he be recalled and publicly flogged, but Othman refused them point-blank. Worse, he threatened to punish them for daring to make such a demand, and when they then appealed to the leading Mother of the Faithful for support, he was heard to sneer in disdain: "Can the rebels and scoundrels of Iraq find no other refuge than the home of Aisha?"

The gauntlet was thrown: a challenge not just to "the rebels and scoundrels of Iraq" but to Aisha herself. As word spread of Othman's sneer, many thought it a foolish thing to have done. Perhaps Aisha had been right in calling Othman a dotard. Perhaps he really was losing his grip, or at least his judgment. Certainly it seemed that way when a respected Medinan elder stood up in the mosque in public support of the Iraqis' demands, and Othman's response was to order him thrown out— so violently that four of his ribs were broken.

If Aisha had been outraged before, she was now incensed. That the guilty should go free and the innocent be beaten? No curtains or veils could stop her. Covering her face in public did not mean muffling her voice, not even—particularly not—in the mosque. The following Friday she stood up at the morning prayers, brandishing a sandal that had belonged to Muhammad. "See how this, the Prophet's own sandal, has not yet even fallen apart?" she shouted at Othman in that high, piercing voice of hers. "This is how quickly you have forgotten the *sunna*, his practice!"

How could Othman have underestimated her? But then whoever would have thought that a mere sandal could be used so effectively? As the whole mosque erupted in condemnation of the Caliph, people took off their own sandals and brandished them in Aisha's support. A new propaganda tool had made its first powerful impression, one not lost on all the caliphs and shahs and sultans of centuries to come, who would produce inordinate numbers of ornately displayed relics of the Prophet—sandals, shirts, teeth, nail clippings, hair—to bolster their authority.

Othman was left with no option but to agree to Walid's recall. He delayed giving the order, however, and balked at the demand for a flogging. Nobody could be found who was willing to administer the required eighty lashes, he claimed, though this was clearly untrue. Worse, the contrast with his predecessor, Omar, could not have been stronger. Nobody had forgotten that Omar had ordered precisely the same punishment for one of his own sons, who had then died under the lash. Under Omar, loyalty to the principles of Islam had trumped any loyalty to family—a principle now utterly undermined by Othman.

Merely recalling his half brother was no longer enough. Letters calling for stronger action traveled the desert routes between Arabia, Egypt, and Iraq, and among them, fiery broadsides from Aisha. Writing in the name of all the Mothers of the Faithful, she called on true Muslims to defend Islam against injustice and corruption. The response took even her by surprise. Within weeks, three columns of heavily armed warriors had arrived in Medina: one each from the garrisons of Kufa and Basra in Iraq, and one from the garrison of Fustat in Egypt, just south of what would eventually be the city of Cairo.

These were no "provincial riffraff." They were several hundred of the best of the Muslim military, led by men of impeccable lineage who left no doubt as to what they wanted: Either Othman took decisive action to address their complaints, or he should resign. Most prominent among their leaders was the son of the first Caliph—Aisha's own half brother Muhammad Abu Bakr. The boy whose widowed mother had married Ali was now grown to manhood, but with neither the judgment nor the patience of his father or his stepfather. Under his orders, the three armed columns did not disperse on arrival to stay with family in Medina but demonstratively set up camp in the dry riverbeds just outside the oasis, on full military alert.

All of Medina waited tensely to see what would happen. Was a coup d'état in the works? Would there be an attack on the palace, even on the Caliph himself? Surely that was unthinkable; Muslim did not kill Muslim, after all. And indeed, despite their militant posturing, the rebels—for that is what they surely were—held back from immediate action. Instead, they reached out to Ali, the one man who had proven his commitment to unity above all else.

For two weeks, Ali acted as mediator. No matter that one side was headed by his own stepson, whose demands he fully endorsed; he was horrified by the younger man's rashness in resorting to armed threat. No matter either that the other side was headed by a Caliph whose style of leadership was the antithesis of everything Ali believed in; he had sworn allegiance to Othman, and allegiance he would give. His would be the role of the honest broker, his ultimate loyalty to neither side, but to the good of Islam, and he might well have succeeded were it not that every step he took was undercut by Othman's cousin and chief of staff, Marwan.

Marwan was known as Ibn Tarid, the Son of the Exile, at least when his back was turned. The exile in question was his father, who had been a leading Umayyad opponent of Muhammad's. When Muhammad had conquered Mecca, he had given all the Quraysh a last chance to be accepted into the Islamic fold as full members of the community. The sole exception he made was Marwan's father, whom he so distrusted despite his last-minute avowal of faith that he ordered him banished along with his family to the mountain city of Taif. Both Abu Bakr and Omar had kept the order of exile in place, but when Othman became Caliph, he had revoked it and called his young cousin to Medina to serve as his chief of staff. It was a position of enormous power, and one that Marwan lost no time taking advantage of.

There was the huge bite he took for himself out of the war booty from the conquest of Egypt, for example, or the matter of how he leveraged the market on animal feed to his own advantage. A canny operator with an eye always on the main chance, he would finally claim the caliphate for himself forty years later, but only for a year. After he had married the widow of the man he had deposed, she and her servants would trap him in his own bed, piling all their weight on top of him until he suffocated—an ignominious death that would give great pleasure to many in the telling.

Under Othman, however, Marwan was in the ascendant. Every approach to the aging Caliph, every financial decision, every piece of information, had to come through him. Nobody said so much as a word to Othman without his say-so. People had the impression of an increasingly frail leader so overwhelmed by the demands of empire that he preferred to retreat into the solitary work of scholarship. Othman spent most of his time compiling the authorized version of the Quran, they'd say, and so was unaware of the degree to which his ambitious kinsman was subverting his authority. Whether this was really so, or whether it was politically wiser to blame Marwan instead of Othman himself, is another question.

Meanwhile, with the rebels camped outside the city, it was Marwan who argued most forcefully against any concession to their demands. That would only encourage further mutiny in the provinces, he insisted. With almost deliciously hypocritical righteousness, he urged Othman to stay the course and not be intimidated, however wrong he might be. "To persist in wrongdoing for which you can ask God's forgiveness," he said piously, "is better than penitence compelled by fear." And in demonstration of his point, he went out to the rebel encampment and let loose with a tirade that seemed designed only to provoke.

"What is the matter with you that you assemble as though for plunder?" he yelled. "May your faces be disfigured! You have come wanting to wrest our property from our hands. Be off from us! By God, if that is what you want, you will not praise the outcome. Go back where you belong, for we shall not be deprived of what is ours."

It was a measure of Ali's success in urging restraint that Marwan was driven off by curses instead of arrows, but such restraint could not last, and Ali knew it. He managed to warn Othman. Marwan was making it impossible for him to act effectively as a mediator, he said, and he could take no responsibility for what might happen if Othman did not put his foot down and rein in his cousin. But the Caliph would hear nothing of it, not even when his favorite wife, Naila, seconded Ali, trying to make her husband see the danger of Marwan's advice. Was it loyalty to family, or was he really in his dotage? Nobody knew, and by now it hardly mattered.

Three days later, when Othman next appeared in the pulpit of the mosque for Friday prayers, he was greeted by jeers and catcalls. One respected elder had even brought along props for emphasis. "Look," he shouted at Othman, "we've brought you a decrepit she-camel, along with a striped wool cloak and an iron collar. Get down from the pulpit so that we can wrap you in the cloak, put the collar on you, and put you on the camel. Then we'll carry you off to the Mount of Smoke"—the main garbage dump of Medina, smoldering with decomposing trash—"and leave you there."

And with that, to drive the message home, the crowd began to fling pebbles at the pulpit, a hail of them aiming hard and true, striking the aging Caliph and knocking him unconscious.

For the Caliph to be stoned unconscious, and in the mosque itself? This was surely full-scale rebellion, an invitation to the harshest of reprisals, as Marwan had urged. Yet even as he was recovering from the stoning, Othman steadfastly refused to order the use of force. Whatever his sins, he said, he was a devout Muslim, and as such, he was determined that no Muslim blood be shed at his order. Yet with equal determination, he refused to resign. Perhaps he really did not grasp the extent of what was happening, or perhaps he truly did believe that he was the deputy not of Muhammad but of God. He hadn't the right to resign, he maintained. "I cannot take off the robes in which God has dressed me." And with this, he signed his death warrant.

The question was who would write that warrant, for it did indeed exist. It took the form of what came to be known as the Secret Letter, lying in wait to be discovered just when it looked as though the crisis had been defused and open conflict averted.

After that stoning in the mosque, Othman had appeared truly shaken and chastened, professing profound regret at having let things develop to such a pass. Now at last he acknowledged the justice of the rebels' demands and pledged not only to dismiss the two most controversial of his governors—his half brother Walid in Kufa and a brother-in-law in the Egyptian garrison of Fustat—but to appoint Ali's stepson Muhammad Abu Bakr the new governor of Egypt. Moreover, lest anyone doubt the sincerity of this pledge, Ali would stand as its personal guarantor.

If one could hear a city sigh with relief, it would have been Medina at that moment. The crisis had been averted, and justice achieved. With Ali's word as their pledge, the rebels struck camp and set off on the long ride back to their garrisons. All might have been well if just three days into their journey back to Egypt, the young Abu Bakr and his men had not seen a messenger riding full tilt behind them, evidently intent on overtaking them.

They stopped and questioned the messenger, and when they realized he was in the service of the Caliph, they searched his saddlebags. There they found a heavy brass inkpot of the kind used by professional scribes, with ink powders and mixing bottles set into a solid base, and compartments for parchment and quills, knives, and seals. One of these compartments was a secret one, however, and inside it they found a letter stamped with Othman's personal seal and addressed to his brother-in-law, the governor of Egypt he had just pledged to replace.

All the leaders of the returning rebels were to be arrested instantly, the letter instructed. First their hair and beards were to be torn out—a calculatedly emasculating form of punishment when so much male pride was vested in long hair and ample beards—and then they were to be given one hundred lashes each. If any still survived, they were to be thrown in prison.

What more was needed? With the written evidence of double-dealing in their hands, the rebels turned around. Three days later they were back in Medina, and this time they didn't merely camp on the outskirts. In no mood to negotiate, they surrounded the palace and placed it under siege.

The seal on the letter was clearly Othman's. Indeed, he acknowledged as much when faced with it. But the letter itself? He swore he'd had absolutely no knowledge of it. Nobody knew for certain if this was the truth or merely plausible deniability. Some were convinced he was lying, while some saw the hand of Marwan at work, even claiming that the letter was in his handwriting. Others argued that it made no difference whose handwriting it was; the Caliph's seal was on the letter, they said, and if his seal could be used without his knowledge, he had no right to his position. Eventually, it was even rumored that it was Ali who had arranged for the letter to be planted and discovered in order to bring about Othman's downfall—and said too that this rumor had itself been planted by Marwan. There was room enough in the story to support any number of conspiracy theories. Only one thing was certain: the secret letter was the end of Othman.

The rebels were not intent on murder—not at first, at least, since they chose to besiege the palace, not to storm it. Though a few did call for outright *jihad* against the Caliph, even they could never have had any intention of beginning the long succession of assassinations that would blight the coming centuries of Islamic history and continue to blight it today. There was still horror at the idea of Muslim killing Muslim, let alone the Caliph.

What they wanted was the very thing Othman refused to give them: his abdication, immediately. There was no longer any room for negotiation. Ali had tried his best, but as the guarantor of the agreement betrayed by the secret letter, he had been double-crossed as badly as the rebels themselves. He could see the potential for violence—he even posted his sons Hasan and Hussein, now grown men in their twenties, to stand guard at the palace—but he surely knew that with Othman so stubbornly entrenched, there was no more he could do to avert disaster. He spent the coming days in prayer in the mosque.

Aisha must have wished she could do the same, and in her way, she did. She could not have played a more public role in stirring up feeling against "that dotard," but she had never imagined things would go this far. She had used Muhammad's sandal to bring Othman back to his senses, but now he seemed to have lost them completely. How could she have foreseen that secret letter? How had things come to the point where she was on the same side as Ali, of all people? Where her own half brother was now besieging the palace? Where she could in good conscience defend neither him nor the Caliph? The whirlpool of overlapping conflicts and loyalties overwhelmed even her, and as the situation worsened, she reached for a way out. She would leave for Mecca on pilgrimage, she announced—not the *hajj* but the *umra,* the individual "lesser pilgrimage" that could be made at any time of the year.

The moment he heard of her plans, Marwan recognized the danger. Aisha's leaving under such circumstances would be taken as a clear signal to the rebels that she would not stand in their way—a silent but powerful blessing of their position. He slipped out of the palace under cover of darkness and made his way to her house. She could not leave, he argued. She had helped create this situation with those fiery letters and speeches of hers, and now she was duty bound to stay and help resolve it. If Othman had scorned her for sheltering "the rebels and scoundrels of Iraq," he had been wrong; he needed her influence with them now, lest things get completely out of hand.

But it was too little, too late. Just a few weeks earlier, Aisha might have taken a certain pleasure in the Caliph's right-hand man pleading with her. She might have taunted him with his newfound respect for the Mother of the Faithful, and would certainly have found a way to turn the situation to her advantage. By now, however, there was no longer any advantage to be had.

"You're running away after setting the country ablaze," Marwan finally accused her, but Aisha would have none of it.

"Would to God that you and your cousin who entrusts his affairs to you each had a millstone around his feet," she retorted, "because then I would cast both of you into the depths of the sea." And with that, she left for Mecca.

The end began with a rumor. Word spread among the rebels that military reinforcements for the besieged Caliph were on the way from his governor in Syria. The reinforcements never arrived, and nobody knew whether the Syrian governor had ever received such a request, or if he had received it and, for reasons of his own, ignored it. Either way, it made no difference; the very idea of Syrian reinforcements brought things to a head. Rumor did its work, as it always does.

The first fatality was one of the most venerable of Muhammad's early companions. He had limped up to the front of the siege line and there, balancing on crutches, called on Othman to come out onto his balcony and announce his abdication. One of Marwan's aides came out instead. He hurled a large stone at the white-haired elder, hit him in the head, and killed him on the spot. "I, by God, ignited the fighting between the people," he boasted later. Nobody would ever know if he acted on his own initiative or at Marwan's orders.

They were to call it the Day of the Palace, though the melee lasted barely more than an hour. The defenders were vastly outnumbered, and once both Marwan and Ali's son Hasan had been injured, the others fled. A small group of rebels led by Muhammad Abu Bakr made their way upstairs and into the Caliph's private chambers. There they found just two people: Othman and the Syrian-born Naila, his favorite wife.

The elderly Caliph, undefended, was seated on the floor, reading a parchment manuscript of the Quran—the authorized version he had devoted years to compiling. Even as the group closed in on him, he kept calmly reading, as though the Holy Book could protect him from mere mortals. Perhaps this was what so infuriated the young Abu Bakr: Othman's assumption of invulnerability even as he was plainly so vulnerable. Or perhaps violence had been building so long that by now it was simply inevitable.

Abu Bakr was the first to strike, the son of the first Caliph leading the assassins of the third. His dagger slashed across the old man's forehead, and that first blood was the sign that released the others. As Othman fell back, they piled in on him, knives striking again and again. Blood splashed onto the walls, onto the carpet, even onto the open pages of the Quran—an indelible image of defilement that still haunts the Muslim faithful, both Sunni and Shia. Yet still they attacked, even after there was no breath left in Othman's body.

Naila flung herself over her dead husband. She begged the assassins not to desecrate his corpse, only to have her blood mixed with his as yet another knife slashed down and cut off part of her right hand. Her dreadful wail of pain and outrage bounced off the blood-spattered walls to pierce the consciences of the attackers; only then did they stop.

Muhammad Abu Bakr had struck the first blow but not the fatal one. There would never be any definitive answer as to exactly whose hand did that. But the question that was to haunt Islam was not who held the knife but who guided it. Who was behind it? Or rather, who was not? One Umayyad later said that Othman was killed by "a sword drawn by Aisha, sharpened by Talha, and poisoned by Ali." Others would say that it was Marwan who both drew the sword and poisoned it. Yet others that it had all been engineered from afar by Muawiya, the powerful governor of Syria, whose rumored reinforcements never arrived.

All that can be said for certain is that the third Caliph was assassinated by persons both known and unknown, with both the best intentions and the worst.

The torn and blood-stained shirt Othman had been wearing when he was killed was to have a long life. After the assassination, someone— nobody is sure exactly who—had the foresight to take it, together with Naila's severed fingers, and wrap the remains carefully for a journey. The next morning, as all of Medina buzzed with the news that the rebels had acclaimed Ali as the new Caliph, a small, somber caravan set out on the seven-hundred-mile ride to Damascus, and in one of the saddlebags, they carried with them that shirt and those fingers.

Was it the Syrian-born Naila who had sent them? Or Marwan? Or

Umm Habiba, the only Umayyad among Muhammad's widows and the sister of the Syrian governor, Muawiya? Whichever it was, the purpose was clear: the grisly relics would serve as a powerful call for revenge. When they arrived, Muawiya ordered them displayed in the main mosque in Damascus, and there they would remain for a full year.

"The shirt was placed each day on the pulpit," said a Syrian historian. "Sometimes it was draped over it, sometimes it covered it, and Naila's fingers were attached to its cuffs—two fingers with the knuckles and part of the palm, two cut off at the base, and half a thumb. The people kept coming and crying at the sight, and the Syrian soldiers swore an oath that they would not have relations with women or sleep on beds until they had killed the killers of Othman and anyone who might try to stop them."

In Medina, Othman was buried quickly and quietly—not by Muhammad's side in Aisha's former chamber, as his predecessors had been, but in the main cemetery. If there was any mourning, it was done privately. In public, the whole of Medina was jubilant. Led by the rebels, they turned to Ali as their new leader. They would have nobody else. The man who so many insisted should always have been the heir to Muhammad had finally come into his inheritance, his ascendance surely all the sweeter for the length of the wait.

On June 16 in that year 656, they crowded into the mosque and spilled out into the courtyard to pledge allegiance to him. The years of dust and thorns seemed finally over—not just for him but for them all.

How were they to know that dust and thorns are not shaken off so easily? They had no idea that Ali would rule for only five years. They rejoiced, applauding the new Commander of the Faithful when he refused to take the title of Caliph. That title had been honored by Abu Bakr and Omar, Ali said, but it had since been corrupted beyond repair by the Umayyads. Instead, he would be known as the Imam—literally, he who stands in front. On the one hand, it was a modest title, given to whoever leads the daily prayers. On the other, this was Imam with a definite capital *I*, the spiritual and political leader of all Muslims. And between Caliph and Imam, a world of politics and theology would intervene.

Ali was destined to be the only man aside from Muhammad himself whom both Sunnis and Shia would acknowledge as a rightful leader of Islam. But while Sunnis would eventually recognize and respect him as the fourth Caliph—the fourth and last of the *rashidun*, the "rightly guided ones"—the Shia would never recognize the caliphate at all, not even the first three Caliphs. To them, Ali was and always has been the first rightful successor to Muhammad, designated by him as the true spiritual leader who would pass on his knowledge and insight to his sons, so that they in turn could pass it on to their own sons. Ali, that is, was the first of the twelve Imams who would join Muhammad and his daughter Fatima as the true *Ahl al-Bayt*.

But on that June day, as all Medina lined up to pledge allegiance to Ali, nobody yet thought in terms of Sunni versus Shia. As they pressed their forearms against his and swore to God that his friend was their friend, his enemy their enemy, they thought that divisiveness was at an end. Ali was the one who would reunite Islam. There would be no more greed, no more self-aggrandizement, no more corruption. The stranglehold of the Umayyads had been broken, and a new era dawned. Under Ali, they would return to the true path of the Prophet.

Yet even as they celebrated, as the drums were beaten and the children danced and the women's ululations lifted joy into the air, that bloody shirt and those severed fingers were on their way to the pulpit in Damascus. And Aisha was in Mecca, planning her own course of action.

chapter 8

THE MOMENT SHE HEARD THE DOGS, AISHA KNEW IT FOR AN omen. The sound itself was familiar enough; howls often rang through the desert night as wolves and hyenas and jackals prowled in the dark. It was where they were howling that unnerved her so: the very place Muhammad had warned her of.

As her army filed into the small oasis midway between Mecca and the distant lowlands of Iraq, it had seemed a welcome stop for the night, but when the howling began, she'd asked: "What is this place?" And when she'd heard the answer—"the waters of Hawab"—a terrible fear possessed her.

"We belong to God and to Him we shall return," she screamed— the Islamic formula recited in the face of death. People crowded around her in alarm. "Don't you see?" she pleaded. "I am the one they are howling at. I heard the Prophet say darkly to his wives, 'I wish I knew which one of you the dogs of Hawab would howl at.' I am the one! Take me back! Take me back!"

What had she done? What had she set in motion? For the first time in months, doubt crept into her mind, and once there, it settled in, paralyzing her.

She had still been in Mecca when the news arrived of Othman's assassination—of her own half brother's role in it and, worse still, Medina's acclamation of Ali. Never mind that she had taunted Othman as "that dotard," or that she had brandished Muhammad's sandal at him and openly accused him of betraying the *sunna*. Never mind that her own letters had helped fuel the rebellion against him or even that her most earnest wish had been to toss him into the sea with a millstone around his feet. Whatever she had intended, it was not this. Not assassination, and certainly not Ali as the new Caliph.

A mix of shock and fury carried her straight to the center of the great mosque—to the sanctuary itself, the Kaaba—and there she stood by the sacred black stone set into its corner and raised her voice loud and clear for all to hear, a firebrand speaking in the name of justice.

"People of Mecca," she proclaimed. "The mob of men, the riffraff from the garrison cities, together with boorish Beduin and foreign slaves, have conspired together. They have spilled forbidden blood and violated the sanctity of the sacred city of Medina. This is a heinous crime! A forbidden thing!" And fired up by the Meccans' roars of approval, she went further still. "By God," she declared, "a single fingertip of Othman's is better than a whole world full of such people. Seek revenge for the blood of Othman, and you will strengthen Islam!"

In response, a fervent rallying cry surged up from the crowd: "Revenge for Othman!" If the Mother of the Faithful could call for her own half brother to be put to death for his crime, by God they would support her! If she could place justice above kinship, righteousness above blood ties, by God so could they! In the name of Muhammad, in the name of Islam, they would take revenge for this son of Mecca struck down by the rebels of Medina.

Aisha never paused to question her motives. Carried along on the crest of her own rhetoric, she didn't ask if it was guilt that impelled her—guilt at having left Medina and abandoned Othman to his fate—or outrage that of all people, it was Ali, the man she most loathed, who had been acclaimed as the fourth Caliph. These questions would rise only by the muddy pool of Hawab, and by then it would be too late to turn back. For the moment, the crowd's acclaim was a heady thing, an intoxicating rush that made her feel all the more righteous.

In death, Othman had achieved the grandeur and nobility that so many had accused him of lacking in life. His murder lay at Ali's door, the Meccans said. Ali knew who was responsible—everyone knew—yet word was that he refused to hand over the culprits for punishment. He was sheltering assassins, and that made him as guilty as the assassins themselves. It might as well have been his hand that wielded the knife, said some, and none as pointedly as the ever-wily Marwan, who had fled Medina for a hero's welcome in Mecca as he showed off his flesh wound from the battle for Othman's palace. "If you, Ali, did not strike the murdered man openly," he declared, "you surely struck him in secret."

The poets, quick as ever to seize the spirit of the moment, took up the call. "Your kinsmen, Ali, killed Othman with no *halal* claim to his blood," said one—no right under Islamic law. "That makes you, their leader, Ali, the one to pay," he continued, "and pay you surely will."

By the time Ali's letter demanding Mecca's allegiance arrived and was read out loud in the mosque, feeling against him ran so high that the demand could barely be heard for the catcalls. The whole crowd burst into frenzied roars of approval as one young Umayyad seized the letter, stuffed it in his mouth, chewed it to a pulp, and spat it out in disgust.

Aisha's vendetta was now that of all Mecca, but passion would convert into action only when her brothers-in-law Talha and Zubayr fled Medina to join her. Both had been among the six who had sat in closed caucus after Omar's death, and both had voted against Ali. Both, like Ali, had become vocal critics of Othman's rule, but that did not mean they wanted Ali to take his place. Talha and Zubayr were ambitious men; each wanted the caliphate for himself, and that was what united them.

So what if they had publicly sworn allegiance to Ali just a few weeks before fleeing to Mecca? They now swore that they had been forced into it by the rebels. They had done it at swordpoint, they claimed. Had pledged allegiance "with a withered hand"—no firm grasp of palm against palm and forearm against forearm, but a half-hearted clasp that belied the words of the oath even as it was proclaimed. It had been clear for all to see. "No good will come of this," people had muttered, and when it was done, Talha had been heard to say: "All we'll get from this is a dog poking its nose in the ground, sniffing dung."

But neither Talha nor Zubayr had the backing to claim the caliphate on his own. Both needed the support of their sister-in-law, especially now that she had the whole of Mecca behind her. With her help, they aimed to force Ali to cede the caliphate. Which of them would then claim it was an open question, best left for later; in the meantime, they would work in concert. With Aisha's presence and influence as the leading Mother of the Faithful, they would muster an army against Ali and confront him—not in Medina, where Ali was too powerful, but eight hundred miles away, in Iraq, where Zubayr had supporters in the southern garrison city of Basra. With Aisha in the lead, they could not fail. "You will rouse the Basrans to action, just as you have the Meccans," they told her.

Aisha was not hard to persuade. She could expect nothing—less than nothing—from Ali, but with either of her brothers-in-law as Caliph, she would regain her position at the center of power. Again, she strode to the Kaaba and let loose with fiery rhetoric. "March to your brothers in Basra and denounce Ali," she cried out. "To Basra!"

And now, halfway there, she was beset by the howling of the dogs, and she was the one who'd roused them. The romance she'd found in the desert until the Affair of the Necklace was a thing of the past. She'd been a teenager then, along for the excitement; now she was in her forties, at the head of an army of thousands, and for the first time, she hesitated.

Was she really to lead these men into battle? Surely it would not come to that. The plan was to take Basra without violence, by force of numbers, then move up the Euphrates together with the Basrans to Kufa. Once all of Iraq was theirs, they would join forces with Muawiya, the governor of Syria, whose army had been primed for revenge by the sight of Othman's shirt and Naila's fingers on the pulpit in Damascus. Against that strong a coalition, Ali would have no option but to concede, as he had three times in the past. That was the plan, but why then were the dogs still howling?

For twenty-four hours Aisha sat there by the waters of Hawab, paralyzed by a sense of foreboding. Talha and Zubayr tried to reason with her, to no avail. The dogs were not howling, they said, merely barking, but she scoffed at that. She was being superstitious, they said, and that was forbidden by Islam; but still she refused to move. They tried lying to her. This was not Hawab, they said; that had been a mistake, and this was another place entirely. Yet still the dogs howled, and she knew this was the place. Knew too that these two men had no right to gainsay what the Prophet had said. Even though they were her sisters' husbands, they were not men to be trusted. Hadn't both reneged on their sworn oath to Ali? Both proven themselves not men of their word?

Why then did she not heed the dogs of Hawab? Why did she not insist on turning back instead of going on to Basra? Perhaps the dogs did not howl loud enough, or perhaps it was hindsight that would make them far more ominous than they seemed at the time. But then Aisha would always be very good at hindsight, and thanks to Ali, she'd live long enough to have it.

Ali had indeed rejected the call to punish Othman's assassins. They had, after all, been the first to acclaim him Caliph, and their leader was his own stepson, so while he did not approve of the assassination, neither could he condemn it. "I cannot say if Othman was killed justly or unjustly," he said, "for he was himself unjust." Yet his statement implied approval. If Othman had been unjust—if he had betrayed the *sunna*, as Ali maintained he had, and contravened the law and the spirit of Islam—then the assassins had acted in good faith. Though Ali stopped short of calling Othman an apostate, his reasoning was clear: as with the killing of an apostate, no punishment was called for.

Instead of retribution, Ali called for reconciliation. Revenge was not the way forward, he said. Islam needed to look to the future instead of to the past. That was why he had accepted Talha's and Zubayr's pledges of allegiance, withered hands or no. It was why he still sent letters to Mecca and Damascus instead of troops, demanding allegiance rather than forcing it. Anyone who misunderstood this as a desire to avoid conflict at all costs, as a position of weakness instead of strength, would find himself gravely mistaken.

But if Ali hoped to avoid bloodshed, it was already too late. When the news arrived of the Meccans marching on Basra under the command of Aisha and her brothers-in-law, he was left with no option but to set out from Medina with his own army to stop them. Yet even as he was en route to Basra, the violence had already begun.

Aisha and her brothers-in-law had miscalculated. They had confronted the Basrans with a terrible conundrum of split loyalties, and the townspeople resented its being forced on them. They respected Aisha as the leading Mother of the Faithful and acknowledged the merit of her call for revenge for Othman, but they respected Ali even more. He had replaced Othman's corrupt governor of the former garrison town, and the new governor—a man of integrity, committed to the rule of law— was popular. So the men of the Meccan army were not welcomed with open arms, as they had expected; in fact, they were not welcomed into the town at all. The new governor insisted that they set up camp beyond the town limits. "Let us wait for Ali to arrive," he said—the last thing Aisha and her brothers-in-law wanted.

That night—"a cold, dark night with wind and rain," according to the records—Talha and Zubayr led a raid on the town. They forced their way into the mosque and fought pitched battles with the townspeople, killing dozens of them. By dawn they had taken over the treasury and the granary, where Ali's governor confronted them. "By God if I had enough men, I would not be satisfied until I killed you for those you have killed," he said. "Because you have killed our Basran brothers, your blood is now *halal*—sanctioned—for us. How can you consider the shedding of Muslim blood lawful? Were those you killed last night the ones who killed Othman? Don't you fear God's loathing?" But against an army of such size, the governor was powerless. He was seized and whipped, his hair and beard were torn out by the roots, and he was thrown in jail. All Basra hunkered down, waiting to see what would happen when Ali arrived.

Riders reached him quickly with the news: the town taken, the governor humiliated, townspeople killed. Ali was dismayed; if Talha and Zubayr did not fear God's loathing, he did. "God, undo what they have done and show them their evil," he cried out. "Spare me the killing of Muslims as they have done, and deliver us from people such as they." But he was a realist as well as an idealist; even as he prayed for peace, he prepared for war.

He sent his sons Hasan and Hussein north to Kufa, there to raise an army of reinforcements. Within the week they met him at Basra with a force several thousand strong. There were now some ten thousand troops on each side, and for the next three days the two armies, the one headed by Ali, the other by Aisha and her brothers-in-law, set up camp across from each other on a wide, shallow plain just outside the town.

Would the show of force be enough in itself to deter the Meccans? Ali evidently hoped so, yet as he addressed his newly massed army, his words would prove horribly prophetic. "To set things right is what I intend," he told them, "so that the community may return to being brothers. If the Meccans give us allegiance, then we will have peace. But if they insist on fighting, this will be a split that cannot be repaired. So men, restrain yourselves. Remember that these people are your brothers. Be patient. Beware of rushing into anything without guidance, for if you win the argument today, you may lose it tomorrow."

The nightmare loomed ahead—the one thing they most dreaded, and the one thing that now seemed all but inevitable: *fitna*.

Arabic is a subtle and sinuous language. Like all Semitic languages, it plays on words, taking a three-consonant root and building on it to create what sometimes seems an infinite number of meanings. Even the exact same word can have different connotations, depending on the context. Perhaps the best-known example is *jihad*, struggle, which can be either the inner striving to live the Islamic life and attain a higher level of spiritual consciousness, or the external armed confrontation with those seen as enemies of Islam.

The sensitive Islamic term *fitna* is still more complex. The root is the word for being led astray. It can mean trial or temptation, intrigue or sedition, discord or dissension. It always implies upheaval, even chaos. But the most common meaning is civil war—the most uncivil warfare of all. Tribes, clans, even families split against themselves; cousins and in-laws take opposite sides; brothers may even fight brothers, and fathers, their own sons. *Fitna* is the terrible wrenching apart of the fabric of society, the unraveling of the tightly woven matrix of kinship, and it was seen in the seventh century, as it still is today, as the ultimate threat to Islam, greater by far than that of the most benighted unbelievers.

So as the two armies faced each other across that divide of sandy, rock-strewn soil, even as they sharpened their knives and swords and steeled their nerves, they debated among themselves as to whether they were really ready to commit the ultimate sin: to shed the blood of other Muslims. Every word they uttered was haunted by the fear of division and its consequence, *fitna*.

"Talha and Zubayr swore allegiance and obedience to Ali," said one veteran Basran warrior, "and now they come in rebellion, seeking revenge for the blood of Othman. They have created a split between us."

War was inevitable, retorted another fatalistically. As well ask the Euphrates to flow upstream as to deny this. "Do the people think they can say 'We believe' and then not be tested?"

But such a test? The Meccan troops too were having second thoughts. "We are in a flat, unhealthy land," said one, and there was no denying the aptness of the metaphor, for this was exactly how southern Iraq, this seemingly endless riverine plain with its canals and swamps, mosquitoes and midges, seemed to the warriors from the Hijaz mountains. The air was dense and moist instead of bracingly dry, the blue of the sky pale with humidity. They had followed Aisha only to find themselves out of place, disoriented.

Even Talha had doubts. He sat alone and "flicked his beard against his chest," the gesture of a troubled man. "We were all united against others," he said, "but now we've become like two mountains of iron, each seeking to finish the other."

Others resisted the pressure to take sides. An elderly companion of Muhammad's complained that "there's never before been a situation where I didn't know my next step, but now I don't know whether I'm coming or going." One tribal leader simply left, riding off into the mountains of Persia, saying that if the two armies wanted to kill each other, they could do so without him and his men. His parting words left no doubt what he thought: "I would rather be a castrated slave herding nanny goats with lopsided udders, than shoot a single arrow at either of these two sides."

Many of the Basrans vacillated, unsure which side to support. "No person who has embraced this *fitna* will be able to extricate himself from it," warned one.

"This will lead to worse than what you most hate," said another. "It is a tear that won't get mended, a fracture that will never be repaired."

And a third simply mourned. "The millstone of Islam is out of balance," he said, "and look how it turns unevenly."

But the strongest warning—the one that would echo in men's minds and make them wish they had listened harder—came from Abu Musa, an elderly companion of the Prophet's and a former governor of Kufa under Omar. "*Fitna* rips the community apart like an ulcer," he said. "The winds fan it, from the north and the south, the east and the west. And it will be endless. It is blind and deaf, trampling its halter. It has come at you from a place where you were safe, and leaves the wise man as bewildered as the most inexperienced. He who sleeps through it is better off than he who is awake in it; he who is awake in it is better off than he who stands in it; he who stands in it is better off than he who rides into it. So be wise and sheathe your swords! Remove your spearheads and unstring your bows!"

There was one last hope, and that depended on the three men in command. As twenty thousand men watched with bated breath, Ali rode out between the two armies on his dark bay battle horse, and Talha and Zubayr rode out to meet him. They came to a halt, as one warrior put it, "so close that the necks of their horses crossed over each other." Still on horseback, they talked, and then there was a mass murmur of approval from each side as Ali gave the sign to bring up a tent so that they could continue their negotiations in the shade. They negotiated for three whole days, and as they talked, so too did their men. "Some stood opposite others and some went across to others," one Meccan remembered, "and all we talked about and intended was peace."

There was one person strikingly absent from that tent, however. Aisha took no part in the negotiations, though her agreement was surely necessary. This was the woman who had inspired the Meccan army to march eight hundred miles to this flat, humid plain, the woman who had called on them to take revenge for Othman and in whose name they had gathered. Did she too hope for a peaceful resolution? Did Muhammad's voice still sound in her ears, warning against dissension, or had she forgotten about the waters of Hawab?

If there was to be a battle, she would not be on the sidelines, not this time. She would be at the very center of the fighting, the rallying point for her men. Was she so entranced by the anticipation of it that she hoped, even against her better judgment, that the negotiations would fail? Was she relieved or disappointed when Ali, Talha, and Zubayr emerged from that tent at the end of the third day and gave the signal to stand down? She would never say.

If it was not peace the three men had agreed on, at least it was not war. They had, in effect, agreed to disagree. Each one had sworn that however this was to be resolved, it would not be by force. None of them would give the order to strike the first blow. So in the words of one warrior, "when they retired to bed that night, there was peace. They slept as they never had before, because they were free from what they had been on the point of doing, and had withdrawn their plans for battle."

But while they slept, he continued, others did not. "At the same time, those who had stirred up the question of Othman spent the worst night of their lives, for now they were about to be brought to account. All night they were busy in discussion until they decided on a surprise attack. They kept it secret, slipped out of the camp before dawn, and attacked at first light."

It was never clear exactly who they were. Were they Marwan's men, setting off the fight, as they had the day Othman was assassinated? Were they acting under orders from Aisha, dismayed at Talha's and Zubayr's retreat from confrontation? Or were they simply young hot-heads, as most prefer to believe, primed for battle and with that supreme disdain of youth for death? The accounts are confused, as battle accounts always are. A small group, certainly, but the smallest group can set huge armies into motion. Three or four men can do it easily. The clanging of steel rises from a single sector, curses and battle cries carry through the still air of early morning, and suddenly thousands are involved. In the terror and desperation of battle, there is no time for questions. Who struck the first blow is the last thing on anyone's mind as every man fights for his life.

Perhaps it is enough to say that with two such huge armies face-to-face, with every man fully armed and geared up to fight, outright battle was the only possible outcome. All we know for sure is that nobody would take "credit" this time, not for this battle, not for the thousands who were to die on this October day in the year 656.

And so it began, the first battle in the war that it seemed nobody wanted yet nobody could avoid—the civil war still being fought in the twenty-first century and in the same place it all began, Iraq.

chapter 9

A ROAR WENT UP FROM AISHA'S FORCES AS HER CAMEL WAS LED
onto the field of battle. It was a red riding camel—the best kind, fast and
sturdy—and the canopy set on top of it was draped not with muslin but
with chain mail and, over that, red silk.

The howdah towered over the vast array of horsemen and in-
fantry. More visible than any banner, it was an instant rallying point for
Aisha's men. The most prominent, the most outspoken, and the most
beloved of the Prophet's widows, the one who had cradled his head as
he lay dying, was not merely on the sidelines; she was right here, among
them, right at the heart of battle. Under the command of the Mother of
the Faithful, there was nothing they would not do.

Through the chinks in the chain mail, Aisha had a clear view of the
whole field. She could see where her lines were doing well and where
they were being pressed, call for one sector to be reinforced or another
to advance. Her commands were relayed by runners to Talha, who was
in charge of the horsemen, and to Zubayr, at the head of the foot soldiers.

As the red silk fluttered over her armored canopy, her high voice pierced through the early-morning air, all the more chilling for being disembodied, its source hidden from sight. "You are heroes, by God. You are like mountains!" she urged her warriors. "Show your valor, sons of mine! Show these murderers what you can do! May they rue the day they were born! May their mothers be bereaved of them!"

And again and again, the urgent refrain: "Death to the killers of Othman! Death to all who support them! Revenge for Othman!"

This was the traditional role of women in battle, though never before from the center. Usually they stayed at the rear, where they urged on their side, mocking the virility of their enemies and daring their own fighters to feats of valor. Their shrill ululations were designed to strike fear in the hearts of the other side, much as the eerie sound of bagpipes in a very different part of the world. They cut through the funk of fear and overrode the sounds of bodies colliding, of steel clashing, of men panting in each other's grip, gasping as steel entered flesh, moaning as they lay injured and dying.

It was women who called for blood, and if any doubted what they were capable of, people still talked with awe of the aristocratic Hind, whose husband had led the Meccan opposition to Muhammad and his followers. Her father had died in the first major battle between the Meccans and the Medinans, and she knew who had killed him: Muhammad's uncle Hamza. So when the Meccans marched on Medina to do battle again, it had been Hind who led the chanting, taunting Muhammad's men and daring them to advance; Hind who had been fired up with the thirst for revenge and who put a price on Hamza's head; Hind who roamed the battlefield after the two sides had fought to a standoff, who strode from corpse to corpse, searching for the one she wanted.

She found it, and when she did, she uttered a cry of victory that years later still froze the blood of those who had heard her. She stood astride Hamza, gripped her knife with both hands, and plunged it deep into his body, gouging him open to rip out not his heart but something far larger and far more visceral—his liver. Ululating in triumph, she held that liver up high above her head and then, in full view of all, she crammed it into her mouth, tore it apart with her teeth, spat out the pieces, stamped on them, and ground them into the dirt.

Who could ever forget the sight of that blood running from her mouth and streaming down her chin and her arms, of those eyes gleaming with revenge? It was so compelling that people still referred to her son, half in taunt, half in admiration, as the Son of the Liver Eater. Never to his face, though, for he was none other than Muawiya, the man who had become the powerful governor of Syria. Like his mother, he was not one to be trifled with.

Yet even Hind had stayed in the rear during the fighting itself. Even she had been too much the urban aristocrat to ride into the thick of battle. That was the kind of thing nomadic women were known for: women like the fabled Umm Siml, who had led her tribe in fierce resistance against Abu Bakr's forces during the Wars of Apostasy. Poets still celebrated her in long odes to the romance of the desert. They praised the sacred white camel she had ridden on and the absolute fearlessness and devotion she had inspired in her men until both she and the camel were finally slain. But Umm Siml had not been a Muslim—not by Abu Bakr's reckoning, in any case. She had been an apostate. So when Aisha rode out onto that battlefield outside Basra on her red camel, it was the first time a Muslim woman had led men into war. It was also to be the last.

Nobody doubted her right to be there, not at the time. Her critics raised their voices only later. "We fought for a woman who thought herself the Commander of the Faithful," said one survivor bitterly. Said another: "Instead of trailing her skirts at home, she crossed the desert at a gallop, making herself a target her sons had to defend against spears and arrows and swords." It is not hard to imagine how the same phrases could be turned around in odes of praise to her courage and leadership, all the more if she had been victorious, or if she had been killed in battle like Umm Siml, but that was not to be.

. . .

What Aisha saw from the height of her camel was a battle as horrific as all had feared. Hardened warriors swore the rest of their lives that they had never seen so many severed arms and legs. It lasted from early morning to midafternoon, and by the time it was done, three thousand men, most of them from Aisha's army, lay dead and dying.

The survivors told their stories, as survivors must. Some chose the path of inspiration, heroic tales of sangfroid in the face of death, like that of the warrior who used his own severed leg as a weapon. The leg had been cut off by a huge sweep of his opponent's sword, and his own sword was gone. He knew that he was done for, but he seized the severed leg, swung it with lethal force at the very man who had cut it off, then collapsed from loss of blood, his head on his enemy's chest. That is how a fellow warrior found him just before he died. "Who did this to you?" he asked.

The answer came with a smile: "My cushion."

Such tales of indomitable spirit in the face of death are legion. Men fight on bravely despite the loss of arms and legs. They fight with their hearts, defying inevitable odds. They fight to the last drop of their own blood, holding their swords in their teeth if need be, as would Hussein's half brother Abbas twenty-five years later at Karbala, when he became one of the great heroes of Shiism. But nobody denies that such tales are a matter of bravado, and everyone knows bravado for what it is: an attempt to ward off terror. That is why most of the stories of the Battle of the Camel forgo heroics for a palpable sense of folly, of the senselessness and tragedy of it all. Each account, each teller, acted as another voice in a vast Greek chorus of tragedy, testifying to the awful bitterness and waste of civil war.

This was hand-to-hand fighting—eye-to-eye fighting, that is, and the eyes they looked into were often those of people they knew. The division between Ali's forces and Aisha's cut deep into the social order. Tribes were divided against themselves that day, and within the tribes, clans and families were split between the two sides, so that cousins, blood brothers, even fathers and sons fought each other.

There was none of the cool distance of modern warfare, where technology reigns and nobody sees the eyes of the enemy or hears the screams. Hand-to-hand combat was utterly and horribly visceral. When they grappled too close to use swords or daggers, they used whatever they could instead. Two fingers jabbed in the eye here. A knee to the genitals there. A rock to the head. An elbow in the kidneys. Warrior after warrior told of the bite of steel into flesh, the acrid smell of blood spouting from severed arteries, the terrifying, unholy, god-awful messiness of combat, with men soiling themselves in fear, with the stink of guts ripped out, with the wild-eyed panic of horses, the blind frenzy of humans, and the sheer bloody-minded desperation of each and every one to find some way, any way, to end the day alive.

Talha and Zubayr were both dead by noon. Talha had taken command of the cavalry and fought valiantly. He might even have prevailed if he had not been shot in the back by an arrow—shot, that is, by someone on his own side. Word was that this someone was none other than Marwan, and indeed, he later admitted as much. Justifying himself with the most pious argument, he pointed out that since Talha had been one of Othman's leading critics, encouraging the rebellion that led to assassination, his claim to be fighting in the name of revenge for Othman was hypocrisy. Thus Marwan, by his own account, had been merely the instrument of justice.

As always when it came to Marwan, there were those who suspected otherwise. Some said he had seized the opportunity to pick off a rival for the caliphate, since if Aisha's side had won the day, Talha would have been declared Caliph, frustrating Marwan's own ambitions. Others said that he had deliberately hung back until he could see which way the battle was going and had then targeted Talha in a misguided attempt to ingratiate himself with Ali. Yet others were convinced that he had acted under orders from a far more powerful rival for the caliphate, for no sooner was the battle lost than he rode across the desert to Damascus, to become a senior counselor in the court of Muawiya, the governor of Syria. One would need a mind as devious as Marwan's to know where the truth lay.

Zubayr's death was another act of treachery, though it would remain unclear exactly whose treachery it was. Word had it that no sooner had the battle begun than Zubayr left the field and started on the road back to Mecca. A clear matter of cowardice, some said, though given Zubayr's record as a warrior, that was hard to believe. A matter of honor, said others, since Zubayr had been in dismay when the truce he had worked so hard to achieve had been so abruptly broken. He had given his word to Ali that his side would not start the fighting, yet now his word had been broken, and he had taken this all the harder since he had already gone back on his word to Ali after swearing allegiance to him, and regretted it. If he had not been a man of honor before, he would be one now, and die for it.

The Meccans would claim that Beduins, always unreliable in Meccan eyes, had chased after Zubayr and killed him as a deserter. But at whose orders? There were rumors of the hand of Marwan at work once again, making sure that both Talha and Zubayr were safely out of the way of his own ambitions, but there was never any proof. It would take Zubayr's son many years to redeem his name.

With both Talha and Zubayr dead, Aisha's battle was lost. All that was left for her to do was give the order to retreat. Yet still she urged her men on, still she uttered her war cries—the high-pitched curses, the chanted taunts—rallying her men around her red camel. It was as though she could not acknowledge even the idea of defeat, or was so carried away by her own rhetoric that she was blinded to the bloodshed all around her. Or perhaps she thought she would show them all that she was not afraid, that she was as courageous as they, that she had what it took. She would never surrender. She would fight to the bitter end.

The battle was reduced to an intense huddle of a few hundred of her men around the camel. One by one, warrior after warrior stepped up to take hold of the camel's nose rein, holding the animal steady to prevent it from bolting from the tumult. One by one, they stood defenseless, with the rein in one hand and her banner in the other, and one by one, they were cut down.

Each time one was killed, another came to take his place. Each time another came, Aisha asked who he was, and he announced himself: his given name, his family, his clan, his tribe. Each time she acknowledged his lineage, called him noble, praised his courage, and watched through the chinks in her chain mail canopy as he too was killed.

Ali's soldiers shouted to her men to surrender, pleaded with them even. There was no battle left to fight, they yelled, no point in this stubborn self-imposed slaughter. But their pleas went unheeded, perhaps even unheard by men deaf to reason, and the deaths around her camel would be laid at Aisha's door. She called herself the Mother of the Faithful, people would say, but what kind of mother would call on her sons to sacrifice themselves this way?

"Oh Mother of ours, the most uncaring mother we know," one poet later wrote. "Did you not see how many a brave man was struck down, his hand and wrist made lonely?"

"Our Mother brought us to drink at the pool of death," wrote another. "We did not leave until our thirst was quenched. When we obeyed her, we lost our senses. When we supported her, we gained nothing but pain."

Seventy men were cut down as they held the reins of Aisha's camel, their bodies strewn at her feet. But if she looked on in horror at the slaughter, she gave no indication of it, and if she was terrified for her own life, she never let anyone know. She certainly heard the arrows thudding into her armored howdah; there were so many of them stuck in the chain mail, one warrior remembered, that it "bristled like a porcupine." Did that armored canopy insulate her somehow from the bloodshed? Did it dull the sounds of death? Was she deaf and blind to suffering, or bravely willing to die for her beliefs? Then, as ever, which Aisha you saw depended not on the facts but on politics.

There is no knowing how many more men might have been killed holding the camel's rein if Ali had not ridden up to put a stop to it. He could see that any demand for surrender was pointless; Aisha's men were too caught up in the heroics of self-sacrifice to hear reason. Yet it was just as clear that if this went on, Aisha herself would be killed, and her death was the last thing he could permit. Whatever he thought of her, she was still the leading Mother of the Faithful.

"Hamstring the camel!" he shouted. "If it's hamstrung, it will fall, and they will disperse!" And the sudden leap of reason spurred one of his men to slip through the cordon of Aisha's defenders and slash at the tendons of the camel's rear legs.

An agonized bellowing filled the air. It took everyone by surprise, as though after all the terrified trumpeting of horses, the cries and howls of men on the attack or falling to their deaths, the clash of steel on steel, the unending stream of curses and taunts from the howdah, the last thing they expected was to be rooted to the spot by the maiming of a single animal. "I have never heard a louder sound than the bellowing of that camel," one warrior declared, haunted by the memory of it, perhaps because once the bellowing stopped, there was silence.

Ali's men stood staring as the camel teetered for a long moment, then slowly collapsed. When it finally hit the ground, they seemed to regain their senses, rushing to cut the straps holding the howdah in place, then lifting it off with Aisha still inside. There was not a sound from her now that she had been brought down to earth, and the silence from the howdah was almost as unnerving as the noise from it had been before.

They had captured the Mother of the Faithful, but now they hung back, unsure how to proceed. None of them dared approach until Ali gave the order to Muhammad Abu Bakr, his stepson and Aisha's half brother, who shouldered his way through the crowd, strode up to the howdah, and drew apart the armored curtains to ask, "Is all well with you?"

"I have an arrow in me," she whispered, and there it was, embedded in the flesh of her upper arm, the only barb out of the hundreds shot at the howdah that had penetrated the armor. Her half brother reached in and pulled it out, and if the pain of it was terrible, as it surely was, Aisha allowed not so much as a whimper to escape her lips. Even in defeat, her pride would not permit weakness.

Her voice issued calm and clear from inside the howdah as she finally conceded the battle, if not the war. "Ali son of Abu Talib," she said, "you have gained victory. You have put your forces to the test well today, so now pardon with goodness."

"Oh Mother, may God forgive you," he said.

"And you," was her ambiguous reply, but Ali let it pass.

Goodness there would be. Ali ordered his stepson to escort Aisha back to Basra; her wound was to be treated, and she was to be accorded full respect. Only then, as she was mounted on a horse and led away from the field, did she seem to register the full extent of what had happened. "Oh God," she kept saying, "had I but died two decades before this day!" Yet it would never be clear if she said this in shame at her defeat, or in regret for her actions, or in sorrow for the thousands of warriors slain at her command.

Ali stayed behind. As the light faded, he walked the corpse-strewn battlefield, and as he went, he repeated the same phrase Aisha had used:

"Oh God, had I but died two decades before this day!" Deep in dismay and sorrow, he patrolled the field far into the night. His men watched as he stopped at every dead body and prayed over it, both those of his own side and those of Aisha's. Many of them he recognized. He paid tribute to their bravery and grieved for their lives, but above all, he spoke of his horror at the sight of so many Muslims killed by Muslims. "I have healed my wounds this day," he mourned, "but I have killed my own people."

He stayed there three days, making amends in the way only he could. He forbade his men to kill the enemy wounded or captives. These were not apostates but good Muslims, he declared; they should be accorded the utmost respect. Those who had fled were not to be pursued. All prisoners were to be set free after pledging allegiance to him, and the usual spoils of war—— swords and daggers, purses and jewelry—were to be returned. To compensate his own men for the loss of spoils, he would pay them directly from the treasury of Basra.

The enemy dead were buried as honorably as those who had fought for Ali. The hundreds of severed limbs were gathered together and placed with ceremony in one large grave. Only when all that had been done—when each and every one of the thousands of dead had been laid to rest in accordance with Islamic law—did Ali ride into Basra and accept the whole city's renewed pledge of allegiance.

If he had done all he could to ease the inevitable bitterness of defeat for those who had fought against him, he now did even more for the woman who had led them. To demean Aisha in defeat, he insisted, would only be to demean both himself and Islam. Once again, he chose the path of unity over that of revenge. When Aisha had recovered from the wound in her arm, Ali assigned Muhammad Abu Bakr to head a military escort to take her back to Medina, together with a full entourage of Basran women to see to her every need, and as her caravan prepared to leave, Aisha seemed to acknowledge his graciousness—at least in part.

"My sons," she told the Basrans, "it is true that some of us criticized others, but do not hold what you have heard against them. By God, there was never anything between myself and Ali other than what usually happens between a woman and her in-laws. Whatever I have said in the past, he has shown himself one of the best of men."

It was as close as she would ever come to a concession speech. Never mind that despite the apparent meekness, it glossed over the truth. She had reduced a bid for control of a vast empire to the level of a mere family squabble, and, in so doing, had surely belittled the thousands who had given their lives for it. Moreover, if she seemed to imply that she accepted Ali as Caliph, she had avoided actually saying so. But Ali could see that this was as far as she would go; there was nothing to be gained by pushing for more. "By God, men," he said, "she has spoken the truth and nothing but the truth. She is the wife of your Prophet now and forever." And together with his sons Hasan and Hussein, he did her the honor of riding alongside her for the first few miles of the route back to Medina.

Aisha accepted all this as her due, but on that long journey back to the Hijaz mountains and the shelter of home, she surely knew that she had suffered far more than a single defeat in battle. If Ali had accorded her honor in defeat, his aides had been less inclined to goodness. She would have many years yet to mull the words of one of his cousins, who had marched uninvited into the house where she was recuperating in Basra and let loose with a torrent of vituperation.

It was she who had incited the people against Othman, he reminded her. Brandishing the Prophet's sandal the way she had? That was an insult to everything Muhammad had stood for. "If you had but a single hair of the Prophet's," he said, "you would boast of it and claim to benefit through it." Worse, by inciting Muslims to battle against other Muslims, she had committed a crime against the Quran, the word of God. But above all, how dare she challenge the *Ahl al-Bayt*, the family of Muhammad?

"We are of the Prophet's flesh and blood," he said, "while you are merely one of nine stuffed beds he left behind. And not the one with the firmest root, or the lushest leaves, or the widest shade."

How horrible for the defeated Aisha to hear herself described as just another of the Prophet's wives, and in such crude terms. For the woman who had always insisted on her unique closeness to Muhammad, this was the ultimate humiliation. And how awful to have her childlessness—no root, no branches, no leaves—thrown in her face yet again, and under such circumstances. This she would never forgive, or forget.

chapter 10

Now, surely, was the golden moment for Ali, the moment he and his supporters had waited for. After the stunning victory of the Battle of the Camel, his position seemed unassailable. Yet he must have sensed that the prize he had thought rightfully his all along had begun to turn to dust from the moment he first held it in his hand. He had been Caliph for four months and would remain Caliph for only another four and a half years.

As the early Islamic historians told the story of his brief rule, it would achieve the epic dimensions of classical tragedy. The story they told was that of a noble leader brought low by his own nobility. Of a man of integrity undone by his reluctance to compromise his principles. Of a ruler betrayed as much by the inconstancy of his supporters as by the malice of his enemies. And all of it fated to be, for the tragic flaw was there from the beginning.

Ali had gained the caliphate under tainted circumstances. They were circumstances beyond his control, to be sure—he had done all he could to prevent Othman's assassination—but they were tainted nonetheless. No matter the twenty-five years he had sacrificed for the sake of unity within Islam, or his spiritual insight, or the justice of his cause. However great his determination to avoid the nightmare of dissension—of *fitna*—the nightmare had caught up with him, and engulfed him.

History had turned on him with a horrible irony. Beware of what you wish for, they say, and that thought surely haunted him as he roamed the battlefield after his victory, praying over the corpse of each warrior and wishing he had not lived to see this day. He had pardoned Aisha with goodness—would have done so even if she had not asked—but all the goodness in his nature had not saved him from what he most feared. Worse still, it would now work against him, for though Ali did not know it, he had only just begun to fight the real war.

All the while, a far more formidable opponent had been merely biding his time. In Damascus, Muawiya had stood calmly by as Ali had been drawn into civil war. The grisly relics of Othman's assassination still hung on the pulpit of the main mosque as he had ordered, serving as all too vivid testimony to the original sin of Ali's rule. But Muawiya saw no reason to take action as long as there was a chance Aisha would do his work for him. Now that she had been defeated, however, he decided to play his hand. He made the cool calculation that if Ali had displayed great nobility of purpose in dealing with Aisha, that same nobility could also serve to hasten his undoing.

The slinky sinuousness of the four drawn-out syllables of the name—Mu-a-wi-ya—seems almost tailor-made for the Shia curses that would be heaped on it in centuries to come. Yet though he would become the Shia epitome of evil, Muawiya may well have been the one man with the political skill and power to keep Islam from falling apart after Ali's death. Certainly he was no one-dimensional villain, though it is true he looked the part. He had a protruding stomach, bulging eyes, and feet swollen by gout, but as though in compensation for his physical shortcomings, he was possessed of an extraordinary subtlety of mind. If he lacked Ali's virtues, he had instead the inordinate advantage of strategic skill and political adroitness.

He ran Syria smoothly—"there is nothing I like better than a bubbling spring in an easy land," he was fond of saying—but it took a certain brilliance to make it look so effortless. By his own account, Muawiya was "a man blessed with patience and deliberateness"—an expert dissimulator, that is, with a positively Byzantine sense of politics that allowed him to turn things to his advantage without seeming to do so.

"How far does your cunning reach?" he once asked his top general. The proud reply—"I have never been trapped in any situation from which I did not know how to extricate myself"—set up the perfect trump card for Muawiya, who countered: "I have never been trapped in any situation from which I *needed* to extricate myself."

Eight centuries before Niccolò Machiavelli wrote *The Prince*, Muawiya was the supreme expert in the attainment and maintenance of power, a clear-eyed pragmatist who delighted in the art and science of manipulation, whether by bribery, flattery, intelligence, or exquisitely calculated deception. His father, Abu Sufyan, had been the wealthiest and most powerful of Mecca's traders and had owned valuable estates and mansions in the rich trading hub of Damascus long before Muhammad had his first Quranic revelation. And though Abu Sufyan had led the Meccan opposition to Muhammad, his son's family ties extended even to the Prophet himself. After the *fatah*, the "opening" of Mecca to Islam, Muhammad had brought Muawiya close in a demonstration of unity. His eighth wife after Khadija's death had been Umm Habiba, Muawiya's sister, and he had appointed her brother to the coveted position of one of his scribes, so that Muawiya could tell of being among those present in Aisha's chamber in the days that Muhammad lay dying. If no others remembered him being there, it was certainly not in their interest to say so.

He had originally been appointed governor of Syria by the second Caliph, Omar, and was then reconfirmed by Othman, not the least because he was Umayyad kin—a second cousin, in fact. But he was also extraordinarily capable. By the time Ali was acclaimed Caliph, Muawiya had ruled Syria for close to twenty years, and the whole province—nearly all the land now known as Turkey, Lebanon, Syria, Jordan, Israel, and Palestine—had become his own personal fiefdom, a powerhouse in its own right.

Until now any role he had played in determining the caliphate had been behind the scenes. Certainly there had been rumors about his involvement in Othman's assassination. Had that secret letter that so incensed the rebels been planted by Marwan on Muawiya's orders? Had Muawiya deliberately withheld the reinforcements requested by the besieged Caliph? Whether there was any truth to such rumors would always remain unclear, and that was the way Muawiya liked it. If they were to be proved true, they would assign power to him; if proved untrue, they would underline his integrity and loyalty to his cousin. So why acknowledge or deny? Either way, rumor played to his advantage. If people wanted to see him in the role of puppet master, staying behind the scenes and pulling the strings, so be it. It established him as a man it was always unwise to ignore.

For the meantime, he had seemed content to consolidate his position and wait patiently, and he had done so in luxury. His palace in Damascus—known as al-Khadra, the Green One, for its distinctive green-marbled facing—was finer by far than Othman's in Medina, yet there was none of the resentment against him that Othman had seemed to inspire, perhaps because Muawiya was known for his generosity as much as for his ruthlessness. In fact, he prided himself on being exactly as generous and precisely as ruthless as he needed to be.

"If there be but one hair binding someone to me, I do not let it break," he once said. "If he pulls, I loosen; if he loosens, I pull." As for any sign of dissent: "I do not apply my sword where my whip is enough, nor my whip where my tongue is enough."

His displeasure, when it was roused, was not a dictatorial wrath, but something far more subtle and, because of that, far more chilling. As one of his senior generals put it, "Whenever I saw him lean back, cross his legs, blink, and command someone 'Speak!' I had pity on that man."

Yet Muawiya accepted with equanimity the one thing that might have displeased him most, and that was his nickname, Son of the Liver Eater. He certainly recognized the taunt in it, for it was an insult for any man to be known by his mother's name instead of his father's, as though he had been born out of wedlock. But he purposely let it ride. "I do not come between people and their tongues," he said, "so long as they do not come between us and our rule." After all, why ban the nickname? The famed image of Hind cramming Hamza's liver into her mouth worked to his advantage. Any son of such a mother could inspire not just fear but respect, and Muawiya commanded both. Except from Ali.

From the moment he had been acclaimed Caliph, Ali was intent on a clear and radical break with Othman's regime. To that end, he'd ordered Othman's provincial governors to return to Medina, and they all had, with the sole exception of Muawiya. The only response from Damascus had been an echoing silence. Muawiya had no intention of being deposed by Ali. In fact quite the reverse.

Ali's aides warned that Muawiya would not fall into line unless he was reaffirmed as governor. Rather than threaten him, they said, Ali should play politics. Leave Muawiya in place and sweet-talk him with promises, they urged, and they would take matters from there. "If you persuade him to give you allegiance, I will undertake to topple him," one of his top generals had promised. "I swear I will take him to the desert after a watering, and leave him staring at the backside of things whose front side he has no idea of. Then you will incur neither loss nor guilt."

Ali would have none of it. "I have no doubt that what you advise is best for this life," he retorted. "But I will have nothing to do with such underhanded schemes, neither yours nor Muawiya's. I do not compromise my faith by cheating, nor do I give contemptible men any say in my command. I will never confirm Muawiya as governor of Syria, not even for two days."

Yet by the time the Battle of the Camel was won, four months had passed; Muawiya was still governor of Syria, and he still had not pledged allegiance. By the time he finally replied to Ali's demands for obedience, he was openly hostile. "Ali, be firm and steady as a fortress," he wrote, "or you will find a devouring war from me, setting wood and land ablaze. Othman's murder was a hideous act, turning the hair white, and none can settle it but I."

Ali's response, as Muawiya had intended, was fury. "By God, if Muawiya does not pledge allegiance, I will give him nothing but the sword!" he swore, even as his aides counseled caution.

"You are a courageous man," said one, "but you are not a warmonger."

"Do you want me to be like a hyena cornered in his lair, terrified at the sound of every loose pebble?" Ali retorted. "How then can I rule? This is no situation for me to be in. By God, I tell you, nothing but the sword!"

Yet his aide had read him well. Ali was the best kind of warrior, one who hated war. Especially civil war. He had fought the Battle of the Camel, proving his determination no matter how high the cost, but he had not chosen that battle and had done all he could to avoid it. And now, despite his anger, he would do all he could to avoid further bloodshed, trusting that Muawiya shared his horror of civil war.

In time some would say that this was naive on Ali's part, even foolish. Others would say that he was misled by his own sense of honor, and that his hesitation in taking military action against Muawiya was that of an upright man confronted with a man who was anything but. But then hindsight is always wise. All that can be said for certain is that in the standoff between Ali and Muawiya, right may have been on one side, but political adroitness was on the other. Only faith could imagine that the former would prevail.

Hoping to pressure Muawiya into obedience, Ali led his battle-tested army north out of Basra to Kufa, a hundred and fifty miles closer to Damascus, and prepared for a long stay. The message was clear: if Muawiya wanted a confrontation, the whole of Iraq would be against him.

The former garrison town of Kufa was now a thriving city on the banks of the Euphrates, with villas built by Othman's administrators lining the river. But Ali refused to take up residence in the former governor's mansion. Qasr el-Khabal, he called it, the Castle of Corruption. Instead, he made his headquarters in a modest mud-brick house alongside the mosque. There would be no more green-marbled palaces, no more favoritism of cronies and kin, no more profiteering at public expense, he declared. He would restore the rule of righteousness, and the Kufans loved him for it.

With the Caliph in residence, Kufa became the effective capital of the Muslim empire. Its inhabitants were no longer "provincial rabble" and "boorish Beduin." They were at the heart of Islam, and Ali was their champion. The burgeoning city had drawn in freed slaves, peasants, traders, and artisans, attracted to Kufa as people still are today to rapidly expanding cities: by the prospect of opportunity, real or illusory. Persians and Afghans as well as Iraqis and Kurds, most of them were converts to Islam, but until now they had been considered second-class Muslims. Under Ali, they were welcomed as equals. The Arabism of Omar and the Umayyadism of Othman were things of the past. Ali, the closest of all men to the Prophet, would lead a return to the ideal of a more perfect union of all believers.

Ali never intended the move to Kufa to be a permanent one. His plan was to return to Medina as soon as he had settled the issue with

Muawiya and Syria, but he never would return. From the moment he made the decision in favor of Kufa, Muslim power began to leave Arabia behind, and this was entirely Muawiya's doing. By refusing to recognize Ali as Caliph, he had forced the issue. It was his defiance that had brought Ali to Kufa and that would lead to Iraq's becoming the cradle of Shia Islam.

Yet it was perhaps inevitable that sooner or later the center of Islamic power would move out of Arabia, and nowhere more naturally than to Iraq. The fertile lowlands between the Tigris and the Euphrates, together with the rich grazing of the Jazeera steppes to the north, had traditionally been the true heartland of the Middle East. The great cities of ancient renown—the Sumerian city of Ur, a hundred miles downriver from Kufa; the Assyrian capital of Nineveh, near Mosul in the north; Babylon, some forty miles north of Kufa; the Persian jewel of Ctesiphon, close to modern Baghdad—all had been in Iraq. Now this land was again the geographical and agricultural center of a vast region, its control pivotal, as both Ali and Muawiya were highly aware, to control of the whole empire.

To the Umayyad aristocrats of Mecca, however, there could be no worse fate. The power they had wielded under Othman would be utterly lost, while these Iraqi newcomers to Islam would be empowered. For the center of Islam to move from where it belonged, in Arabia? It was an insult, a clear reward to the "provincial riffraff" that so ardently supported Ali. Were Mecca and Medina to be sidelined? To become mere places of pilgrimage, hundreds of miles from the center of power? Were they to be relegated to the status of onlookers in the faith to which they had given birth?

The Meccans' concerns were well founded. Their descendants were to be the Islamic rulers of the future, but they would never live in Arabia. As the centuries passed, Muslim power would center in Iraq, in Syria, in Persia, in Egypt, in India, in Spain, in Turkey, anywhere but

Arabia, which became increasingly cut off, saved from reverting back to its pre-Islamic isolation only by the pull of the annual *hajj* pilgrimage. Arabia would not exert political power again for more than a thousand years, until the fundamentalist Wahhabi sect emerged from the central highlands in the eighteenth century to carry out violent raids against Shia shrines in Iraq and even against the holy places of Mecca and Medina. In alliance with the Saud family, the Wahhabi influence would spread worldwide in the twentieth century and into the twenty-first. Financed by oil wealth, Arabia—now Saudi Arabia—would regain the preeminence it had once held in Islam, aided and abetted by the Western thirst for oil even as it nurtured the Sunni extremists who would turn so violently against the West.

Only one thing remained for Muawiya to put into place, and that was a popular outcry for war against Ali. His position would be far stronger if he could manipulate not just assent to war, but a demand for it. He had kept the pot simmering with the display of Othman's shirt and Naila's severed fingers on the pulpit in Damascus, but now he needed to bring it to a boil. In a move worthy of the most skillful modern spinmeisters, he would steal Ali's sense of honor and adapt it to fit himself instead.

He set about a carefully staged campaign to present himself as loath to take action. He would have to be forced into it by the outraged conscience of the people. If he declared war on Ali, he would then merely be obeying their will, the humble servant of his people and their demand for justice.

The first line of attack in this campaign was poetry. This is certainly a strange idea in the modern West, where poets are so easily ignored, but in the seventh-century Middle East, poets were stars. Especially satirical poets, whose work was endlessly quoted and chanted. It was written not to be read but to be memorized and repeated, to make the rounds not of literary salons but of the streets and the alleys, the marketplace and the mosque. The more cutting the verses and the sharper the barbs, the more popular and irresistibly repeatable they were, and the more renowned their creators.

They were taken with sometimes deadly seriousness. When one popular poet opposed Muhammad's ascent to the leadership of Medina—"Men of Medina, will you be cuckolds allowing this stranger to take over your nest?" she'd taunted—she had received a sword through her heart in the dead of night for her pains. Word spread as quickly as her poems had, and other Medinan wordsmiths who had been critical of Muhammad quickly began turning out verses in his praise.

In the twenty-first century, Westerners shocked at the scope of Muslim reaction to Danish cartoons of Muhammad seemed to conclude that there is no tradition of satire in Islam. On the contrary, there is a strongly defined tradition, and one clearly linked to warfare. In the seventh century, satire was a potent weapon, and it is still seen that way. Salman Rushdie's novel *The Satanic Verses* created such a stir in the Islamic world because it was an extraordinarily well-informed satire. By playing on Quranic verses and on *hadith* reports of Muhammad's life, Rushdie cut close to the bone. While satire may be thought relatively harmless in the West—at its best, cutting-edge humor, but the cut only a figurative one—in Islam the cut is far more literal. When they are the first weapon in war, words draw blood.

Satire was usually aimed at the enemy, however. It took a mind as subtle as Muawiya's to see the potential in poems that seemingly insulted him, calling his virility into question and accusing him of weakness if he held back from open war with Ali.

Some of these were written, or at least signed, by his cousin Walid, who was also Othman's half brother—the same man who had fueled resentment of the third Caliph with his drunken antics in the pulpit as governor of Kufa. "Muawiya, you have wasted time like a stallion camel in lust, confined and bellowing in Damascus but unable to move," Walid wrote. "By God, if another day passes without revenge for Othman, I would that your mother had been barren. Do not let the snakes come at you. Do not be faint with withered forearms. Present Ali with a war to turn his hair gray!"

Others urged Muawiya to "rise high in the stirrup" and "grasp the forelocks of opportunity." But the most popular of all the verses making the rounds in Damascus was the one that clearly laid out the opposing sides. "I see Syria loathing the reign of Iraq," it went, "and the people of Iraq loathing Syria. Each one hates his partner. They say Ali is our leader, but we say we are pleased with the son of Hind."

Such poems could not possibly have circulated without Muawiya's knowledge and approval. They were an essential part of his campaign to rouse the will of the people to war—a will that was eminently amenable to skillful manipulation. In fact, the will of the public can still be manipulated in much the same way in even the most proudly democratic of countries, as was clear when the Bush administration falsely presented the 2003 invasion of Iraq as a response to the Al Qaida attack of September 11, 2001.

Muawiya's declaration of war came by letter. "Ali, to each Caliph you had to be led to the oath of allegiance as the camel is led by the stick through its nose," he wrote, as though Ali were not himself the Caliph but at best a mere pretender. He accused Ali of inciting the rebellion against Othman "both in secret and openly." Othman's murderers were "your backbone, your helpers, your hands, your entourage. And the people of Syria accept nothing less than to fight you until you surrender these killers. If you do so, the Caliph will be chosen by a *shura* among all Muslims. The people of Arabia used to hold that right in their hands, but they have abandoned it, and the right now lies in the hands of the people of Syria."

In Muawiya's hands, that is. The governor of Syria was ready to claim the caliphate for himself.

Early that summer of 657 the two armies, Syrian and Iraqi, met at the Plain of Siffin just west of the Euphrates, in what is today northern Syria. Ali's army had followed the river five hundred miles north from Kufa in high spirits. The farther they'd ridden, the clearer the air had become, free of the humidity that hung over the lower Euphrates. The rich alluvial valley gradually narrowed. Desert bluffs gave way to the high grazing lands of the Jazeera with snow-covered mountains to the north, and the silt-laden river that had eddied wide and brown at Kufa ran strong with the end of the snowmelt.

If they prevailed, all Syria lay before them, and its crown, Damascus, with its enormous wealth. They had heard tell of the lushness of Damascus—the canals, the trees, the exotic fruit, the Green Palace with its marble forecourts and gem-encrusted thrones and bubbling fountains. The very idea of fountains! Clear, fresh water in such lavish abundance that it could be used for mere amusement? This was worth fighting for.

Thousands of armed men do not march hundreds of miles to make peace, yet once they reached Siffin, it was a matter of honor to each side that it be seen as the injured party, not the aggressor. For weeks, then, they held back, engaging only in duels and skirmishes. Even these almost ritualized encounters were strictly limited, for when the time for prayer arrived, as it then did three times a day, the warriors separated and moved half a mile apart to pray. "As night fell," one of them remembered, "we would ride into each other's camps and sit down and talk."

Their commanders talked too. An ornate canvas pavilion was erected between the two armies, with the banners of both sides fluttering from each corner. Here Ali's and Muawiya's envoys tested each other's determination. But Muawiya had a clear advantage in such talks: he was fully aware of Ali's horror of civil war, and now sought ways to make this work to his advantage. After all, there were other, less costly means than outright war to achieve his aims.

Even as he publicly demanded that Ali resign as Caliph, Muawiya instructed his envoys to quietly propose an alternative solution. He and Ali should avoid war by agreeing to divide the empire between them, he said. He would take Syria, Palestine, and Egypt and all the revenue from them, and Ali would retain control of Iraq, Persia, and Arabia. A de facto partition of the empire, that is, along the very lines that had divided the Byzantine and Persian empires before the Arab conquest, and in effect, two Caliphs instead of one.

It came as no surprise when Ali indignantly turned down the idea, but even if the proposal was bound to fail, it served as yet another means of taunting him. Ideally, it might even prompt him into attack so that Muawiya would then seem the injured party, and Ali the aggressor. Instead, Ali made one last effort to avoid all-out battle. He rode up to the pavilion at the center of the plain and called out Muawiya, his voice carrying to the front lines of either side as he challenged the Syrian governor to a one-on-one duel that would decide the whole matter and save mass bloodshed.

Muawiya's chief of staff, Amr, the famed general who had conquered Egypt for Islam, urged him to accept the duel. "It is not fitting that you refuse such a challenge," he said with the military man's code of honor. "Ali has made you a fair offer."

But Muawiya was more than content to leave honor and valor to Ali. His concern was far more practical. "It is not a fair offer," he retorted. "Ali has killed everyone he has ever challenged to single combat." And with this refusal, the only option left was battle.

Ali turned back and addressed his troops. "The Syrians are fighting only for this world, that they may be tyrants and kings in it," he said. "If they are victorious, they will pervert your lives and your faith. Fight them now, or God will take the rule of Islam away from you and never bring it back!" As his men cheered him on, he called on them to display all the ferocity of those who had been grievously wronged. "Fight the enemy," he said, "until their foreheads are split by shafts of iron and their eyebrows are dispersed over their chins and their chests."

This time there would be no breaks for prayer and no riding into each other's camp to talk things over. The Battle of Siffin lasted three days, and the fighting was so intense that it continued right through the second night. The Night of Shrieking, they were to call it, for the unearthly howls of men in mortal agony, a sound more fortunate people now know only as that of an animal hit by a car, dragging itself to the side of the road to die.

Ali himself was nearly killed. Arrows fell so thick and fast around him that as one witness said, "his two cubs, Hasan and Hussein, were hard put to fend off the shafts with their shields." They urged Ali to move faster so as to avoid being so exposed. His famed reply, the epitome of heroic sangfroid in the face of battle, was an augury of what was to come.

"My sons," he said, "the fateful day will inevitably come for your father. Going fast will not make it come later, and going slow will not make it come sooner. It makes no difference to your father whether he comes upon death, or death comes upon him."

But death would not come upon Ali at Siffin. As the sun rose on the Friday morning, the field was all but won. The Syrian line was not holding, and the Iraqis were slowly but inexorably advancing, despite their losses. It was only a matter of time—another few hours at most—until Ali's forces could claim a definitive victory, or so it seemed.

Amr persuaded Muawiya that what could not be won by might could nonetheless be won by guile. Unburdened as Muawiya was by any aspiration to spiritual leadership, he should feel free to make whatever he saw as the best use of faith. So the command was given: not to retreat, and certainly not to surrender, but to bring several parchment copies of the Quran. These were distributed among Muawiya's top cavalry, with orders for each horseman to spear a single parchment sheet on the tip of his lance and then ride into the enemy lines. Instead of waving the white flag of surrender, Muawiya would wave the Quran.

No white flag could have been more effective than the sight of those parchment leaves fluttering atop the enemy lances. Stop fighting, in the name of God, was the message. Do not shed blood on the leaves of the Holy Book. As Muslim men, put up your arms. And in case any missed the message, the Syrian cavalrymen cried out the words Muawiya had ordered them to use: "Let the Book of God be the judge between us!"

Ali was stunned by such gall. Even to think of placing the Quran on lances was blasphemy. Surely his own soldiers could see this for what it was, a ruse, pure and simple. "They have raised up the Holy Book only to deceive you," he yelled at his troops. "All they want is to outwit you and trick you."

But if half the men could see that, the other half could not. "When we are called to the Book of God," they said, "we must answer the call. We cannot fight against the Quran itself." And despite orders to the contrary from their commanders, they laid down their weapons. On the verge of victory, Ali could only watch as it was snatched away.

"By God," he fumed at his men, "I tell you that you have been cheated!" But reason was no weapon against faith. The image of Othman's blood-stained Quran was still fresh in the men's memory; they were not about to commit sacrilege again.

Muawiya quickly sent up a herald to stand between the two armies and read aloud his proposal for how they should proceed. The issue of who should be Caliph, he said, should be resolved not by men but by God, not by battle but by the Quran itself. Each side should pick its most trusted representative to sit in arbitration and resolve the issue, using the Quran as his sole guide. The final judgment would thus be that of God alone.

The proposal drew cheers from Ali's men, for Muawiya had deliberately couched his proposal in the most pious terms. Besides, it seemed clear to them that any arbitration guided by the Quran could only favor Ali. But Ali himself was not deceived. The very idea of arbitration to decide who was to be Caliph not only placed his own right to the caliphate in question from the start, it also made the Quran itself a matter of negotiation. For the first time, the Quran was being made into a political tool.

Ali had been thoroughly outmaneuvered. No matter that he could plainly see how Muawiya had manipulated the situation, or that one of the most worldly of men had used faith as a weapon against one of the most spiritual. With his troops standing fast by their refusal to fight any further, Ali was left no option but to consent to arbitration. "Do not forget that I forbade you this," he told his men. "This will only demolish strength, destroy right, and bequeath lowliness. Shame on you! You are like cowardly she-camels rooting in the muck for scraps. You will never again see glory!"

It was less than a year since he had been acclaimed Caliph in Medina, yet here, on the Plain of Siffin, he surely sensed that his reign would not be a long one. He had been on the brink of winning the battle, and now had begun to lose the war.

chapter *11*

A DISPIRITED IRAQI ARMY FOLLOWED ALI ON THE LONG JOURNEY
back to Kufa. Many of the men had begun to second-guess their eager-
ness to accept arbitration at Siffin. Perhaps they realized that they had
indeed been duped, and their faith used against them, because none were
more bitter than those who had most stoutly insisted on laying down
their arms when they had seen the Quran on the lances of Muawiya's
cavalry. And since Muawiya was by then back in Damascus, they took
out their bitterness on the man who had led them to Siffin in the first
place.

Blaming Ali for the very act they had forced him into, they would
form an entirely new kind of enemy, not from Mecca or from Syria but
from within his own ranks—an enemy all the more dangerous since they
were fueled not by the desire for power but by the blind, implacable
logic of embittered righteousness.

Their leader was Abdullah ibn Wahb, a name that still reverberates
in the Islamic world since it calls to mind Abd al-Wahhab, the founder of
the fundamentalist Wahhabi sect that today holds sway in Saudi Arabia
and is the ideological backbone of Sunni extremism. To his followers,

the seventh-century Wahb was known as Dhu'l Thafinat, the Scarred One. Some said this was because of the dark callus on his forehead, a sign of extreme piety created by repeated bowing down in prayer, others that it was because his left arm was deformed from battle wounds. Either was reason enough to hold him in awe.

When Ali ascended the steps of the pulpit to give his first sermon back in Kufa, Wahb began to berate him. "You and the Syrians have vied with each other in unbelief like two horses in a race," he declared. "God's ruling on Muawiya and his followers is that they should repent or be killed, yet you have made an agreement with them to let men decide. You have given men authority over the Book of God, and so your deeds are worthless, and you are lost!"

His followers joined in. The role of Caliph could not be arbitrated, they shouted. The succession to the Messenger of God was a matter of divine right. That right had been Ali's, but he had now forfeited it. He was as guilty as Muawiya of transgressing divine law. There was no difference between the two; both were equally abhorrent in the eyes of God. And again and again, they shouted out the slogan that was to become their rallying cry. "Judgment belongs to God alone!" they cried. "To God alone!"

"Those words are true," Ali countered, "but you twist them and use them to mean something false." It was they who had insisted that he agree to arbitration at Siffin, he said. They had ignored his warnings then; how could they now attack him for doing what they had insisted on?

But there is nobody as righteous or as blind to reason as the reformed sinner. "When we wanted arbitration," Wahb replied, "we sinned and became unbelievers. But we have repented. If you now do the same, we will be with you. But if you will not, then as the Quran says, 'We reject you without distinction, for God does not love the treacherous.'"

As the rest of the mosque rose in uproar over the idea of Ali as a traitor to Islam, Wahb declared that the whole of Kufa was mired in a state of *jahiliya*, the pagan darkness that had reigned before the advent of Islam. "Let us go out, my brothers, from this place of wicked people," he said, and go out they did, some three thousand strong. Fifty miles north of Kufa they established a new settlement on the Tigris at Nahrawan. It was to be a haven of purity, Wahb announced, a beacon of righteousness in a corrupt world.

He and his men were to be the first Islamic fundamentalists. They called themselves the Rejectionists—*khariji*, meaning "those who go out." The reference was to the phrase "those who go forth to serve God's cause" in Sura 9 of the Quran, which is aptly titled "Repentance." They had seen the light and repented, and with the absolutism of the newly penitent, they devoted themselves to the letter of the Quran and to the exclusion of its spirit. We are holier than thou, they were saying, purer than the pure. And as is the way with such righteousness, they took their zeal for purity over the brink into all-out fanaticism.

Anything that fell short of their standard of faith was nothing less than apostasy and had to be ruthlessly rooted out lest it contaminate the righteous. They began to terrorize the countryside around Nahrawan, submitting everyone they caught to a kind of mini Inquisition. If the answers failed to satisfy their rigid standards, the punishment was death.

Matters came to a head when they chose the farmer son of an early companion of Muhammad's as their victim. A number of them had ridden into his village for supplies and decided to make an example of him. Since his father had been among those who had warned against taking sides before the Battle of the Camel, they posed a loaded question. "Did your father not tell you that the Prophet told him: 'There will be a *fitna* in which the heart of a man will die as does his body, and if you are alive then, be not the slayer, but the slain'? Did he not say that?"

That was indeed what the Prophet had told his father, the farmer replied, even as he trembled in fear, for it was clear that a refusal to take their side was the utmost betrayal in the eyes of these men and that he himself was about to be not the slayer but the slain. Yet as they closed in around him, he took a brave last stand. "Ali knows far more of God than you do," he said.

With that, he sealed his fate. Ali was an apostate in Rejectionist eyes, and anyone who submitted to the rule of an apostate was himself guilty of apostasy, and his life forfeit. They leaped on the farmer, tied him up, and dragged him together with his pregnant wife beneath the heavily laden date palms of an orchard next to the river.

The details of what happened next are tellingly precise. At one point, a date fell to the ground, and one of the Rejectionists picked it up and put it in his mouth. "You do that without the owner's permission and without paying for it?" said the leader of the band. "Spit it out!" Then another began to swing his sword in threatening circles and by chance hit a cow that had wandered behind him, killing it. At this, the others insisted he go find the owner and pay him the animal's full value. They waited while he did so, and then, having acted with the utmost righteousness in the matter of both the date and the cow, they meted out due punishment. They made the farmer kneel and watch as they disemboweled his wife, cut out the unborn infant, and ran it through with a sword. Then they cut off the farmer's head. "His blood flowed like the lace of a sandal," swore one witness. Justice thus upheld—the date spit out, the cow paid for, the farmer and his wife butchered—they purchased their supplies and went on their way back to Nahrawan.

They did so with the clearest of consciences. Even the murder of the wife and unborn child, they maintained, was called for by God, since women and children of the enemy shared in the sin of their male kin. There were no innocents. And in this, the seventh-century *khariji* Rejectionists set the pattern for their descendants.

Like his forerunner the Scarred One in the seventh century, Abd al-Wahhab would "go forth" with his followers into the desert highlands of central Arabia eleven centuries later. There, near what is today the city of Riyadh, he set up a spartan, purist community uncontaminated by the pagan darkness and corruption he claimed was rife in

Mecca and Medina. As had the Rejectionists, the Wahhabis soon raided far and wide out of their desert stronghold. Early in the nineteenth century, they destroyed the domes over the shrines of Fatima and others in Medina, and even damaged the Prophet's own tomb. Such ornate shrines were idolatry, they said, and rode on north into Iraq, where they ransacked the shrines of Ali and his son Hussein in Najaf and Karbala.

The Wahhabis' impassioned call for a return to what they saw as the purity of early Islam gathered strength in the twentieth and twenty-first centuries, not only in Saudi Arabia but also in such movements as the Taliban in Afghanistan, the Salafis in Egypt, and Al Qaida. The perceived enemy within Islam would become as dangerous as the enemy without, if not more so. Like the Egyptian president Anwar Sadat, who was assassinated in 1981, any leader who dared negotiate with an enemy, let alone make peace, was declared the archenemy, and headed the list of those to be eliminated.

Among Iraqi Shia today, the word "Wahhabi" still serves as shorthand for all forms of Sunni extremism, no matter their countries of origin. The power politics of the Iraq civil war have been played out against a millennium and a half of Shia memories of intolerance and barbarity, all leading back to that scene by the Tigris of the butchering of a farmer and his pregnant wife, and to the spectacle of a rightful Caliph in Kufa accused of betraying the Quran by the men who had insisted that he lay down his arms in its name.

For Ali, the slaughter under the date palms was beyond contempt. He sent a message to Wahb demanding that he surrender the killers. "As the Quran says, 'Indeed, this is clear depravity,'" he wrote. "By God, if you had killed even a chicken in this manner, its killing would be a weighty matter with God. How will it be, then, with a human soul whose killing God has forbidden?"

Wahb's reply: "All of us are their killers. And all of us say: Your blood, Ali, is now *halal*—permitted—for us."

It was an outright declaration of war, in words that still chill the blood of anyone who hears them in the Muslim world. They are the words of implacable righteousness, of those who kill without compulsion, in the name of God. For the third time, Ali was left no choice but to do the one thing he most abhorred: lead a Muslim army against other Muslims.

When they reached Nahrawan, it was quick and bloody. The Rejectionists hurled themselves against Ali's vastly superior forces, seemingly regardless of any concern for their own survival. "The truth has shone forth for us!" they cried to one another. "Prepare to meet God!"

And an ominous precursor to the cry of modern suicide bombers: "Hasten to Paradise! To Paradise!"

Only four hundred Rejectionists survived, though it might have been better for Ali if there had been no survivors at all. More than two thousand martyrs were created that day, and as is the way with martyrs, their memory would inspire yet more.

The man who had sacrificed so much to avoid *fitna* had now fought three civil war battles. In all three, he had been victorious—or would have been if his men had kept fighting at Siffin—but he could not escape a growing feeling of self-loathing. He had waited twenty-five years for this? Not to lead Islam into a new era of unity but to kill other Muslims?

"Since I became Caliph," he told his cousin, "things have gone continually against me and diminished me." If it were not for the need to stand up against corruption and oppression, "I would throw off the bridle of leadership, and this world would be as distasteful to me as the dripping from the nose of a goat."

With Muawiya working against him, however, the diminishment would only continue. As was his style, the Syrian governor continued to

undermine Ali at every turn. "After Siffin," he later said with great satisfaction, "I made war on Ali without armies and without exertion."

The arbitration agreed on at Siffin took almost a year to set up.
There were all the usual diplomatic preliminaries: the need to agree on
an agenda; to determine the size and makeup of the delegations from
each side; to agree on the timing of the conference, the format, and the
location, a small town halfway between Kufa and Damascus. Yet when
all the details were in place and the two sides finally met, it would end
only in further bitterness.

Muawiya was represented by his chief of staff, Amr, who had conquered Egypt for Islam and was soon to become its governor in reward
for his work. Ali would have chosen his own chief of staff, the general
who had so vividly volunteered to take Muawiya to the desert "and leave
him staring at the backside of things whose front side he has no idea of,"
but his men insisted instead on the aging Abu Musa. This was the man
who had argued so strongly that they should remove their spearheads
and unstring their bows before the Battle of the Camel. "*Fitna* rips the
community apart like an ulcer," he had said then, and now that the ulcer
was eating at them, they remembered his words. Never mind that Ali's
chief aides called Abu Musa "blunt of blade and shallow," a man too easily manipulable by sharper minds. The rank and file countered that "he
warned us of what we have fallen into." They would accept nobody
else.

The conclave lasted two weeks, and at the end, Abu Musa and Amr
stepped forward to make a joint declaration. As Abu Musa understood
it, they had agreed to the perfect compromise: A *shura* would be held to
reaffirm both Ali as Caliph and Muawiya as governor of Syria. That is
what he announced to the hundreds of those gathered for the conclud-
ing ceremony. Then came the double cross.

When Amr stepped up to the podium, his spin on Abu Musa's
words was not at all what the old man had in mind. He and his good

friend Abu Musa had indeed agreed to a *shura,* he said, but its purpose was to confirm not Ali but his opponent as Caliph. "I hereby confirm Muawiya as the true Caliph," Amr concluded, "the heir of Othman and the avenger of his blood."

Curses hurtled through the air, fistfights broke out, and the conclave broke up in more turmoil than when it had begun. Abu Musa fled for Mecca, where he lived out his days in privacy and prayer, utterly disillusioned with public life, while Amr returned to Damascus to lead the acclamation of Muawiya as Caliph.

The year was 658, and there were now two Caliphs. A Caliph and an anti-Caliph, that is, and no agreement on which was which. The odds against Ali were stacked higher than ever, and due to his principled insistence on equalizing the revenues from Islam, they were to become higher still.

Influential estate owners and tribal leaders were accustomed to what they considered the perks of their position. Without these perks, they were open to what Muawiya called "the use of honey"—sweetening the pot. So when Ali refused to make sweetheart deals with the nobility, he paid dearly. Even one of his own half brothers, infuriated by the lack of a special pension, was bribed over to Muawiya's side.

But there were also other uses for honey. Muawiya had his sights set on Egypt, where Ali's stepson, Muhammad Abu Bakr—Aisha's half brother—had proved a weak governor. Ali himself ruefully acknowledged that he was "an inexperienced young man." So when news came that Muawiya was planning to dispatch Amr to take over Egypt, Ali sent one of his most experienced generals to shore up the province's northern defenses. The general traveled by ship from Arabia instead of taking the land route through Palestine so that he could avoid Muawiya's agents, but that was wishful thinking. When his boat docked, he was welcomed with a great show of hospitality by the chief customs officer, a man already well "sweetened" by Muawiya, and offered the customary honeyed drink in welcome.

The poison in it killed him within hours. As Amr would later say, "Muawiya had armies in honey."

Poison has none of the heroics of battle. It works quietly and se-lectively, one might almost say discreetly. For Muawiya, it was the per-fect weapon.

His personal physician, Ibn Uthal, a Christian and a noted al-chemist, was an expert on poisons, as was his successor, Abu al-Hakam, also a Christian. Their records no longer exist, but Ibn Washiya's *Book on Poisons,* written in ninth-century Baghdad as a guide for his son, has survived.

Equal parts biology, alchemy, and superstition, Ibn Washiya's work constituted the state of the art for centuries to come. One section deals with poisons that work by sound. It was thought that certain sounds under certain circumstances could kill, and it may have been this belief that heightened Aisha's terror when she heard the howling dogs at Hawab. Another section details the use of various parts of snakes, scor-pions, and tarantulas, but even seemingly innocuous creatures could be effectively used. If nothing else, the Twenty-third Compound Poison, for instance, was sure to produce death by botulism. It called for "the blood of a decrepit camel" to be mixed with its gall, sprinkled with squill and sal ammoniac, and then buried in donkey manure for a month "until it is musty and covered with something that resembles a spider's web." Two grams of this in food or drink, and death was guaranteed within three days.

If more rapid fatality was desired, it could be induced by cyanide extracted from apricot pits, with the faint almond odor masked in a drink of date juice or goat's milk thickened with honey. Or there were herbal poisons like henbane and deadly nightshade. A particular favorite was monkshood, specifically recommended for use on the blade of a sword or a dagger so that the slightest nick would provide effective entry into the bloodstream of the victim. And by the end of the seventh century, the alchemists of Damascus had developed "inheritance powder"—transparent arsenic, odorless and tasteless, which could be slipped into a drink by anyone seeking to speed up the process of inheritance.

With such an arsenal at his disposal, one can see how Muawiya could boast that he made war on Ali without armies. Honey worked for him and would continue to do so, whether in bribes or in a cooling, fatal drink.

The Syrian army took Egypt with ease. Muhammad Abu Bakr had sent a small force to the border, but they were completely outnumbered, and routed. Dismayed by such ineffective leadership, the rest of his army either fled or switched sides to join forces with the Syrians, and when Abu Bakr himself was hunted down, alone and half dead of thirst in the desert, the Syrian soldiers carried out their revenge for Othman on the man who had led his assassins. Ignoring orders to take Abu Bakr alive, they sewed him into the rotting carcass of a donkey, then set it on fire. Some accounts have it that he was already dead by then; others, that he was still alive and burned to death.

Ali was distraught at the news, and Aisha even more so. As though she had never been alienated from her young half brother, she mourned him at dramatic length—so much so that she provoked one of her fellow Mothers of the Faithful, Muawiya's sister Umm Habiba, into sending her a "condolence gift" of a freshly roasted leg of lamb, dripping with bloody juices. The accompanying message read: "So was your brother cooked." Aisha was violently sick at the sight of it, and, at least by her own report, refused to touch meat again for the rest of her life.

Ali had lost Egypt, and still the attacks kept coming from every quarter. The *khariji* Rejectionists had reorganized and attracted thousands of new recruits not only in Iraq but throughout Persia, where whole cities now ousted Ali's governors and refused to send taxes to Kufa. Syrian units began a long series of harassment raids into Iraqi territory, terrorizing the population and reinforcing the feeling that Ali could not provide even the most basic security. Arabia itself came under attack, yet even after Muawiya had sent a punitive force to Mecca and Medina and on into the Yemen, where thousands of Ali loyalists were summarily executed, Ali could not rouse his once-invincible army to action. Demoralized by the seemingly endless civil war, his men refused to move. "Our arrows are exhausted," they said. "Our swords are blunt, and our spearheads all used up."

The man who had been so famed for eloquence was reduced to haranguing his own fighters, berating them as cowards. "You Kufans are only lions in time of peace, and sly foxes when you are called to be brave," he complained from the pulpit. "May your mothers be bereaved of you! I call you to the aid of your brothers in Mecca and Medina and you gurgle like slack-jawed camels slurping their water. If you hear even a rumor of Syrian horsemen coming against you, each of you hides in his house and locks his door, like a lizard in his hole. Whoever places his trust in you is duped. Whoever draws you, draws a useless lot. You have filled my heart with pus and lined my breast with anger. By God, knowing you has brought in its wake nothing but grief and sorrow. If I did not desire to die in God's cause, I would not remain with you one more day."

And indeed, he had few days yet to come.

It happened at dawn on Friday, January 26, in the year 661, midway through the monthlong fast of Ramadan. Ali had walked to the mosque in Kufa for the first prayer of the day. He never saw the armed man lurking in the shadow of the main entrance, not until the raised sword glistened above him in the early light and he heard the Rejectionist cry coming from his attacker's lips: "Judgment belongs to God alone, Ali! To God alone!"

The sword blow knocked him to the ground and gashed his head open. "Do not let that man escape," he shouted as he fell, and worshipers rushed out of the mosque and caught hold of his assailant.

Ali remained lucid even as the blood ran down his face and people began to panic at the sight. There was to be no call for revenge, he said. "If I live, I shall consider what to do with this man who attacked me. If I die, then inflict on him blow for blow. But none shall be killed but him. Do not plunge into the blood of Muslims saying 'The Commander of the Faithful has been killed!' And do not inflict mutilation on this man, for I heard the Messenger of God say, 'Avoid mutilation, even on a vicious dog.' "

The assassin was executed the next day. Ali's wound had not been fatal, but the poison smeared on the sword had done its work.

Hasan and Hussein washed their father's body, rubbed it with herbs and myrrh, and shrouded it in three robes. Then, as Ali had instructed them, they set his body on his favorite riding camel and gave it free rein. Forty years before, Muhammad had given his camel free rein to determine where the mosque would be built in Medina. Where it stopped, there the mosque was built. Now another sainted animal would determine where Ali would be buried. Wherever it knelt, that was where God intended Ali's body to rest.

The camel went a half day's journey, walking slowly as though it knew its burden and was weighed down by grief. It knelt some six miles east of Kufa, atop a barren, sandy rise—*najaf* in Arabic—and there his sons buried the man who would ever after be revered by all Muslims, but by two very different titles: the first Imam of Shia Islam, and the last of the four *rashidun*, the Rightly Guided Caliphs of Sunni Islam.

"Today, they have killed a man on the holiest day, the day the Quran was first revealed," Ali's elder son, Hasan, said at the graveside. "If the Prophet sent him on a raid, the angel Gabriel rode at his right hand, and the angel Michael at his left. By God, none who came before him are ahead of him, and none who come after him will overtake him."

In time, a shrine would be built over Ali's grave on that sandy rise, and the city of Najaf would grow up around it. Each time the shrine was rebuilt, it grew more magnificent, until the gold-leafed dome and minarets soared above the city, shining out to pilgrims still twenty miles away. By the late twentieth century, Najaf was so large that nearby Kufa had become little more than a suburb hard by the river. All the more canny, then, of Muqtada al-Sadr, the leader of today's Mahdi Army, when he adopted not the Najaf shrine but the main mosque of Kufa as his home pulpit. In doing so, he took on the spirit not of Ali assassinated, but of the living Imam. Preaching where Ali had preached, Muqtada assumed the role of the new champion of the oppressed.

But Najaf was to be only the first of Iraq's twin holy cities. As the Caliph Muawiya assumed uncontested power, the second city was still just a nameless stretch of stony sand fifty miles to the north. It would be twenty years yet until Ali's son Hussein would meet his fate here, and this stretch of desert be given the name Karbala, "the place of trial and tribulation."

Part Three

Hussein

chapter 12

O<small>N THE MORNING OF</small> S<small>EPTEMBER</small> 9 <small>IN THE YEAR</small> 680, <small>A SMALL</small> caravan set out from Mecca, heading for Iraq, and at its head Hussein, Ali's younger son. Nineteen years had passed since he and his brother had buried their father on that sandy rise outside Kufa, then made the long, dispiriting trek back across northern Arabia to the shelter of the Hijaz mountains. Hussein had waited with almost impossible patience as Muawiya consolidated his rule over the empire, but now the waiting was over. Muawiya was dead, and Hussein was intent on bringing the caliphate back where it belonged, to the *Ahl al-Bayt*, the House of Muhammad.

The divisiveness that had begun with Muhammad's death and then taken shape around the figure of Ali had now reached into the third generation. And here it was to harden into a sense of the most terrible wrong—a wrong so deeply felt that it would cut through the body of Islam for centuries to come, with still no end in sight.

Hussein was by now in his mid-fifties, and it surely showed. His beard must have been at least flecked with white, his eyes and mouth etched around with deep lines. Yet the posters that today flood Iraqi and

Iranian markets show an extraordinarily handsome man in his twenties. Long black hair cascades down to his shoulders. His beard is full and soft, not a gray hair to be seen. His face is unlined, glowing with youth, and his dark eyes are soft but determined, sad and yet confident, as though they were seeing all the joy and all the misery in the world, and embracing joy and misery alike.

In the West, the posters are often mistaken for somewhat more muscular images of Jesus, and indeed the resemblance is striking. If Ali was the foundation figure of Shia Islam, Hussein was to become its sacrificial icon. The story of what happened to him once he reached Iraq would become the Passion story of Shiism—its emotional and spiritual core.

Yet as Hussein's caravan threaded its way out of the mountains and onto the high desert, a dispassionate observer might have taken one look and thought that he was almost destined to fail. If his aim was to reclaim the caliphate, this small group seemed pitifully inadequate to the task. The line of camels traveled slowly, for they carried the women and children of his family, with only seventy-two armed warriors for protection and just a few horses tied to the camels by their reins. Nevertheless, the group rode with assurance, confident that once they arrived, the whole of Iraq would rise up under their banner.

At first, that confidence had seemed justified. Letter after letter had been carried across the eight hundred miles between Kufa and Mecca in the weeks since Muawiya had died and his son Yazid had succeeded to the throne in Damascus—so many letters that they filled two large saddlebags, and all of them from the Shiat Ali, the followers of Ali.

"Speed to us, Hussein," they urged. "The people are waiting for you, and think of none but you. Claim your rightful place as the true heir of the Prophet, his grandson, his flesh and blood through Fatima, your mother. Bring power back where it belongs, to Iraq. We will drive out the Syrians under your banner. We will reclaim the soul of Islam."

The pivotal message was the one that came from Hussein's cousin

Muslim, whom he had sent to Kufa to confirm that the Iraqis were indeed committed to his leadership. "I have twelve thousand men ready to rise up under you," Muslim wrote. "Come now. Come to an army that has gathered for you!"

It was the call Hussein had waited nineteen years to hear, ever since his father's death.

Ali had not been the only target the morning he was attacked, or so it was said. Word was that the *khariji* Rejectionists had also planned to kill Amr in Egypt and Muawiya in Syria. But Amr had been sick that day—a stomach ailment, they said—and the cloaked figure struck from behind was only a subordinate. And though the would-be Syrian assassin found the right man, he merely slashed Muawiya in the buttocks, and the newly uncontested ruler of the empire suffered only temporary discomfort.

Few were so rash as to point out how convenient it was that only Ali had been killed, and by Muawiya's favorite weapon, poison. Those few were quickly and irrevocably silenced.

There was even a story that Ali's assassin had carried out the deed for love: to win the hand of a woman whose father and brothers had been among the Rejectionist martyrs killed at Nahrawan. "I will not marry you until you give me what I want," the story has her saying. "Three thousand dirhams, a slave, a singing girl, and the death of Ali the son of Abu Talib." The presence of that singing girl on her list of conditions spoke clearly of a romantic fiction, and no such romance was ever concocted about the men who purportedly attacked Muawiya and Amr. But that was no matter; it was far safer for most Muslims to blame the fanatic Rejectionists, and them alone.

Assassination creates an instant hero of its target. Any past sins are not just forgiven but utterly forgotten. Every word is reinterpreted in the light of sudden loss, and every policy once thought mistaken now seems the only right course of action. Political life is haunted by the sense of what might have been, of an ideal world that might have existed if only the assassination had never taken place. So it is today, and so it was in seventh-century Kufa. The same sword stroke that erased Ali's life also erased all doubts about him. If they had diminished him in life, in death the Iraqis would raise him up as the ultimate authority, almost on a par with Muhammad himself.

The poisoned sword had been wielded by a Rejectionist, but as the Kufans reeled in shock, their sense of outrage was fueled by the conviction that Muawiya had somehow been behind it. Ali had been right all along, they said, and called for nothing less than what they had so stolidly refused before: all-out war on Muawiya.

They surged to the mosque to declare allegiance to Ali's scholarly elder son, Hasan, and demanded that he lead them against Syria. But even as passions ran high all around him, Hasan remained a realist. He accepted the Kufans' allegiance out of a sense of duty but clearly considered it more a burden than an honor. War was pointless, he knew, for the Syrian army was far better trained and equipped than the fractious Iraqi one. And besides, just the thought of a continuing civil war filled him with loathing.

He was haunted by Ali's final bequest, spoken as the poison rapidly spread through his veins. "Do not seek this world even as it seeks you," he had told his sons. "Do not weep for anything that is taken from you. Pursue harmony and goodness. Avoid *fitna* and discord." And finally, quoting the Quran: "Do not fear the blame of any man more than you fear God."

As sons will do, Hasan held his father to account for betraying the principles he had preached. Ali had allowed himself to be dragged into civil war, and Hasan could not forgive him for that. He had admired Othman for his abiding faith in Islam. Had been deeply shocked at the way the aging third Caliph had been so ruthlessly cut down. Had criticized his father's declaration of amnesty for Othman's assassins, and looked on with horror at the escalating bloodshed ever since. More war was the last thing Hasan wanted, and Muawiya, thanks to his vast network of informers, knew it.

Cannily aware that the pen can indeed be as mighty as the sword, Muawiya now sent Hasan a series of carefully reasoned letters. In them, he recognized Hasan's spiritual right to the caliphate but argued that he, Muawiya, was better suited to the task. He was the older man, he said, the more seasoned and the more worldly-wise in an uncertain world. He was the one capable of ensuring secure borders, of repressing Rejectionist terrorism and assuring the safety and integrity of the empire. Much as he admired Hasan's scholarship and piety, much as he honored him as the grandson of the Prophet, the times called for a strong leader—a man of experience and action, not a man of intellect.

And as was his way, he sweetened the pot. If Hasan abdicated his claim to the caliphate, Muawiya would ensure that he was amply compensated, in both the short term and the long. A large payment would be made to him from the Iraqi treasury, along with Muawiya's oath that on his own death, he would name Hasan as the next Caliph.

Hasan was tempted. He knew he was no warrior, and longed for the peace and quiet of days spent studying in the mosque. He could also see how fickle those who supported him could be. He had watched as his father had been diminished in stature by the Iraqis, stymied at every turn. If they now held Ali up as the highest ideal, they could change their minds again just as quickly. Indeed, as he mulled Muawiya's offer, it was the Iraqis who would decide him.

They had gathered for what they thought would be a fiery sermon calling them to war. But Hasan was not the inspirational speaker his father had been. A mild speech defect forced him to speak in a slow monotone, with each word given equal weight. He had gravitas but lacked fire, and this was clear as he took the pulpit to preach not what the people wanted but what he believed: the supremacy of the greater *jihad*—the lifelong struggle within oneself to become the ideal Muslim—over the lesser *jihad*, or armed struggle. If the Kufans counted it shameful to turn away from war, he said, then "shame is better than hellfire." He would seek not war with Muawiya but an honorable peace, and a general amnesty for all past bloodshed.

They were brave words, instantly taken for cowardice. "He is weak and confused," the Kufan warriors shouted to one another. "He intends to surrender. We have to stop him." And the man who wanted nothing more than to prevent further violence suddenly became the object of it. His own men turned on him in a mutinous free-for-all, man-handling him and pulling the robe off his back. A knife appeared—nobody was ever sure whose knife it was—and cut into his thigh. It was not a deep wound, but enough to draw a flow of blood, and that fact probably saved Hasan's life. As he fell to the ground, the sight of the blood sobered the mutineers, and they realized how dangerously close they had come to yet another assassination.

If there had been any doubt in Hasan's mind as to what he should do, it was now resolved. Even if he wanted, he could not lead an army capable of turning on him in this way. Abdication was the only option, and Muawiya's terms seemed reasonable enough. He had sworn that Hasan would succeed him as Caliph. Hasan must have reasoned that if his father, Ali, had waited through the reigns of three Caliphs before taking his rightful place, citing the need for unity, then he himself could surely wait through just this one.

Hussein pleaded with him to reconsider. "I beg you, heed the words of Ali," he said, "not the words of Muawiya." Deception was Muawiya's modus operandi, he argued. Nothing good could come of negotiating with such a man, no matter what he had promised. But a younger brother rarely holds much sway over an older one, and besides, the wound in his leg had already persuaded Hasan.

He was still limping as he mounted the pulpit to address the Kufans for the last time. "People of Iraq, you have pledged allegiance to me, swearing that any friend of mine is a friend of yours," he said. Now he called on them to follow through on that pledge. "I have deemed it right to make peace with Muawiya and to pledge allegiance to him, since whatever spares blood is better than whatever causes it to be shed."

There was utter silence by the time he finished speaking, a silence that held as he descended from the pulpit and left the mosque. He told his brother to prepare for the long ride back to Medina and to do so as quickly as possible. He would be thankful, he said, to see the last of Kufa.

Who could blame him? The Shia certainly do not. In Shia Islam, Hasan is revered as the second Imam, the rightful heir to Ali and so to Muhammad. He had given up the leadership of the empire, but the far more important authority of spiritual power was indisputably his. Hasan, they would say, had placed his faith not in worldly power but in faith itself. Though there were also those who would say that the money certainly helped.

There is no firm record of how much he was given from the Iraqi treasury. There never is in such situations. Some say it was five million silver dirhams, enough for him to return to Medina a wealthy man. But Hussein was to be proved right in warning his brother against Muawiya. Hasan would not have long to enjoy his newfound wealth.

Muawiya, now the undisputed fifth Caliph, entered Kufa with all due pomp and circumstance. He gave the Kufans three days to swear allegiance to him, and did not need to spell out what would happen if they refused. Swear they did on the first day, and with loud enthusiasm.

If their hearts were not his, their self-interest definitely was. And if some would accuse them of being fickle, others would say they were pragmatic. Here at last was the "strongman" they had been yearning for. For all Ali's talk of unity, Muawiya was the one who could actually achieve it—not by the power of faith and principle, as Ali had hoped, but by far more down-to-earth methods.

After five years of civil war, law and order would prevail. The empire that had teetered on the brink of disintegration would be rescued. Muawiya was to rule for nineteen years, and on his death—of natural causes, itself a sign of political stability—his eulogist would call him "the rod and the blade of the Arabs, by means of whom God cut off strife." Whatever part he had taken in creating that strife was not the stuff of eulogies.

With Kufa newly submissive, the man who had mused that "I like nothing better than a bubbling spring in an easy land" now went about assuring himself of just that. He took great delight in the rewards of power, tempered only by a certain ironic sensibility—in many ways a very modern one. It's said that one time, as he watched the arrival in Damascus of a caravan full of Arabian horses and Caucasian slave girls, he sighed with satisfaction at how good the caliphate had been to him. "May God have pity on Abu Bakr, for he did not want this world, nor the world him," he said. "Then the world wanted Omar, but he did not want the world. And then Othman used up this world, and it used up him. But me—I revel in it!"

He did not even mention Ali, editing him out of thought as if he could edit him out of history. But at that point in time, history surely seemed his to write. His was the subtle political mind that had gone up against Ali's elevated spiritual one, and it had been clear to Muawiya from the beginning which of them would prevail, at least in terms of worldly success. One was destined to eat dust and thorns; the other to contemplate his slave girls and thoroughbred horses.

The Iraqis might still have posed a problem. They had sworn allegiance, but Muawiya had no intention of relying on their oaths. These were the people who had pledged themselves to Ali yet disobeyed him, then pledged again to Hasan and turned on him. Muawiya was determined to ensure not their loyalty—he was hardly so foolish as to expect that—but their continued submission. All that was needed was the right man for the job. If the Kufans had been as glad to see Hasan go as he had been to leave them, they would soon change their minds.

Ziyad, the veteran general appointed by Muawiya as the new governor of Iraq, was also one of the toughest. He had once been known as Ibn Abihi—the "Son of His Father"—and the identity of that father had been a matter of both dispute and entertainment. The most consistent rumors had it that Ziyad was a bastard son of Muawiya's father, Abu Sufyan. Some said that his mother had been a concubine of Abu Sufyan's; others swore that she had been a prostitute; yet others that worse still, she had been a Christian, and Ziyad was "the son of a blue-eyed mother." But nobody called him Ibn Abihi any longer, not unless they wanted to be burned alive or crucified or slowly hacked to pieces, limb by limb. Ziyad had a way of making himself understood, even with the most unruly populace.

"Spare me your hands and your tongues," he told the Kufans on taking office, "and I shall spare you my hand and my arm. I swear by God I have many potential victims among you, so let every man of you beware lest he be among them."

The Kufans responded at first with a certain cowed respect. After the civil unrest of Ali's rule, Ziyad at least provided security. In fact he enforced it. "He compelled the people to obey," one Kufan remembered. "If a man or a woman dropped something, none would touch it until its owner came back and picked it up. Women spent the night without locking their doors. And if so much as a rope should be stolen in his realm, he would know who had taken it." Just as Italians reconciled themselves to Mussolini's dictatorship in the 1930s by saying that he "made the trains run on time," so the seventh-century Iraqis accommodated themselves to Ziyad's regime. Even the Rejectionists hunkered down, wary of retaliation.

The price of such security was dread. Ziyad established a secret police network to keep track not only of stolen ropes but also of any emergent opposition. He was as uncompromising as he had promised in response. Collective punishment—uprooting orchards, confiscating land, demolishing houses of relatives of those he suspected—was as effective as it was ruthless. So too was his demand that people spy on one another and name names.

"Let each man save himself," he ordered. "Inform me of troublemakers sought by the Caliph Muawiya. Make lists of them, and you will be free from harm. Anyone who refuses will be denied protection, and his blood and property will be *halal*"—Ziyad's to take at will.

With his secret police, his network of informants, his brutal reprisals, Ziyad ran Iraq much as another dictator was to run it fourteen hundred years later. Like Saddam Hussein, he was a Sunni ruling a majority Shia population. If they pined for Ali, that was their problem. He could not control their hearts, but he could, and did, control their every action. He was every bit as ruthless as Saddam would be, and seemingly as immovable.

Given his purpose, Muawiya had chosen his man in Iraq well, all the more since he had no fear of Ziyad's turning against him. He ensured his new governor's absolute loyalty with the least expensive yet most generous of gestures: the public recognition of Ziyad as a legal son of Abu Sufyan and thus as Muawiya's own half brother. Family ties replaced the stigma of bastardy; nobility dispelled dishonor. So when Ziyad died, victim to one of the seventh century's many localized outbreaks of the plague, it was perfectly natural that his son Ubaydallah, now Muawiya's legal nephew, take his place as governor of Iraq. And just as natural that Ubaydallah prove himself very much his father's son.

With Iraq thoroughly subdued and all overt signs of Shia sympathy quashed, with the trade routes safe and secure, and taxes coming in from as far away as Algeria to the west and Pakistan to the east, life was good for Muawiya. Only one cloud threatened his horizon: his commitment to appoint Hasan his successor as Caliph. It had been necessary at the time, one of those concessions a wise politician makes, but always in the awareness that things change with time. A great leader's worth, after all, was measured by his legacy, and history made it clear that such a legacy was best ensured by founding a dynasty. An Umayyad dynasty, that is, with Muawiya's son Yazid to become Caliph after him.

Muawiya's dynastic ambition was to utterly change the caliphate. On this, both Sunnis and Shia are in agreement. The protodemocratic impulse that had driven the earliest years of Islam—the messy business of the *shura*, with the principle, if not quite the practice, of consensus—would become a thing of the past. As Byzantine despotism had appropriated Christianity, so now Umayyad despotism would appropriate Islam.

Muawiya had already had himself crowned Caliph in a *coup de théâtre* staged in Jerusalem, where he assumed the former role of the Byzantine emperor as guardian of the Christian holy places. Many of his most senior officials were Christians, including Ibn Uthal, his physician, and Al-Mansur ibn Sarjun, the grandfather of Saint John of Damascus. The Byzantine influence was all too clear. The caliphate was to become a hereditary monarchy in what would be seen as the degenerate Persian and Byzantine mold, and Yazid seemed to fit that mold perfectly.

He was the image of a spoiled scion given to drink and dissipation, the antithesis of the Islamic ideal. "A silk-wearing drunkard," Hasan once called him. Even Ziyad, angling perhaps for his own selection as Muawiya's successor, warned that Yazid was "easy-going and neglectful, devoted only to hunting." Muawiya's son seemed to be a kind of seventh-century version of a good old boy from Texas, succeeding his father to the highest office in the land.

But that was to underestimate him, let alone his father. Muawiya would never have appointed a dissipated roué to carry on his legacy. Yazid may have liked his drink, but he had also proved himself an effective administrator and a capable commander in the field. If he was not the Islamic ideal, that was no matter. Muawiya had no intention of making his son heir to the pulpit; he wanted him heir to the throne.

And, Muawiya might have argued, why not? What was so different about the claim of the *Ahl al-Bayt* to the caliphate? Wasn't its claim based on the same principle of blood inheritance, as though matters of the spirit could be passed on by birth along with facial features and the family name? Wasn't the son of the fifth Caliph as entitled to the throne as the son of the fourth? More so, in fact, if the stability Muawiya had achieved was to be maintained?

Besides, it was not as though he would be taking the caliphate away from the family of Muhammad. From the *Ahl al-Bayt*, yes, but wasn't family a larger thing than that? Wasn't he himself the Prophet's brother-in-law? And weren't the Umayyads also the family of the Prophet? Muawiya's grandfather Umayya had been a first cousin of Muhammad's grandfather, making both Muawiya and Yazid distant cousins of the Prophet. They were in a different line of the family, true, but family all the same.

As it happened, Muawiya had no need to make his case. It could simply be considered a matter of perfect timing for him when Hasan died at the age of forty-six, just nine years after returning to Medina. He died of natural causes, Sunnis would say, but the Shia would tell a different story. Muawiya, they charged, had ensured Hasan's early demise by means of his favorite weapon—a honeyed drink laced with poison.

Muawiya had found the vulnerable link, they said. The hand that slipped the fatal powder into the cup was the least expected—one of Hasan's wives, Jaada. She had married the man she thought would inherit the caliphate after his father, Ali, and hoped to be the mother of his sons, the heirs to power. But though Hasan had many sons by other wives, the sons Jaada hoped for never materialized. Neither did the status of marriage to the leader of an empire. After Hasan's abdication, Jaada had found herself part of the household of a revered but powerless scholar in what had become the backwater of Medina. So perhaps she thought that if this husband would not be Caliph, another one could be. Perhaps that was why she had been open to Muawiya's offer.

He had promised lavish payment for her trouble—not only cash but marriage to Yazid, the man he would declare the heir to the caliphate once Hasan was out of the way. And since Muawiya always paid his debts, she did indeed receive the money. But not the son. When the newly self-made widow tried to claim the second part of her reward, Muawiya rebuffed her. "How," he said, "can I marry my son to a woman who poisons her husband?"

Hasan, the second Imam of Shia Islam, was buried in the main cemetery of Medina, though that was not where he had wished his grave to be. He had asked that he lie alongside his grandfather under the floor of Aisha's former chamber in the courtyard of the mosque, but as the funeral procession approached the compound, Muawiya's governor barred the way with troops and diverted the mourners to the cemetery. The last thing Muawiya wanted was to have Hasan enshrined alongside the Prophet. He was all too aware of the potential power of shrines

A different account of Hasan's forced resting place lays the blame squarely at the door of another controversial figure. In the years since the Battle of the Camel, Aisha had become the doyenne of Medinan society, the aging dowager who settled disputes, arranged marriages, and, whenever she needed to, which was often, invoked her memories of life with Muhammad as a means of enforcing her wishes. She seemed to have made her peace with the past, but when she heard that Hasan's funeral procession was heading for the mosque, all the old resentment came surging up again.

The son of her nemesis Ali to lie alongside the Prophet? Under the floor of the chamber that had once been hers and that still legally belonged to her? She could not allow such a thing. She gave orders for a gray mule to be saddled and rode out to intercept the procession as it wound through the narrow alleys near the mosque, stopping it in its tracks. "That chamber is still my property," she announced. "I do not grant permission for anyone else to be buried there."

The crowd of mourners came to a halt, and their numbers soon swelled with others, attracted by the confrontation. Some spoke out in favor of Hussein, who stood by his brother's bier at the head of the procession; others were in favor of Aisha, who sat firm on her mule, unbudging. One of her nephews tried to defuse the situation with humor. "Oh aunt," he said, "we are still washing our beards from the Battle of the Red Camel, and you would now have people speak of the Battle of the Gray Mule?" But as the dispute grew more heated and threatened to get physical, it was Hussein who found a way to save face for all concerned.

It was true that his brother had asked to be buried alongside his grandfather the Prophet, he said, but the request had come with a proviso: "unless you fear evil." Since evil was now to be feared in the form of a fight at a funeral, Hussein gave the order to divert the procession to the cemetery. Instead of being buried alongside Muhammad, Hasan would lie next to his mother, Fatima.

And so it was done. Nobody would ever know for sure whether it was at Muawiya's command or Aisha's insistence, but to place the blame on Aisha was certainly an excellent way to divert it from Muawiya. The bold and irrepressible leader of the Mothers of the Faithful was no longer beyond reproach.

The fire was still there, but only in sparks. "Are you not afraid I will poison you in revenge for the death of my brother Muhammad Abu Bakr?" she once asked Muawiya when he visited Medina and paid her a courtesy call. It was he who told the story, laconically adding the famed comment that "there was never any subject I wished closed that she would not open, or that I wished opened that she would not close." Even in forced retirement, Aisha still commanded respect, however grudging.

These were the years in which she did what retired public figures still do: in effect, she wrote her memoirs, or at least dictated them. She told the stories of her life with Muhammad, many of which are still enshrined as *hadith*—the reports of Muhammad's sayings and practice that would form the *sunna*, taking second place in Islam only to the Quran itself. Aisha told the stories again and again, refining them each time, and if anyone pointed out that her recollections sometimes contradicted one another, she would take a tack familiar to modern politicians. She had misspoken then, she would say, but was speaking correctly now. Or in a still more familiar tactic, she would simply deny ever having said whatever it was she had said before.

Still, retirement did mellow even her. In the years after Hasan's death, with Muawiya clearly bent on turning the caliphate into a monarchy, she seemed to regret her role in taking arms against Ali. "I caused wrongdoing after the Prophet," she acknowledged, and steered clear of politics, contenting herself with the constant flow of visitors, the diplomatic courtesy visits, the gifts and adulation. Yet she must have realized how meaningless all this was. She had been at the center of the story of Islam, and now she was on the sidelines. Times had changed, the empire had changed, and Aisha had little option but to accept being made into a kind of living monument.

Worse still, there were those who would have preferred that she be a dead one. Among the politicians making the obligatory courtesy call on her in Medina was Amr, Muawiya's governor of Egypt and his former chief of staff, who made no bones about the matter. Aisha knew that Amr spoke for Muawiya as well as for himself when he told her to her face that it would have been better for all concerned if she had been killed at the Battle of the Camel. When she asked how so—and only Aisha would even have asked—the answer came with horribly unexpected frankness. "Because then you would have died at the height of your glory and entered heaven," Amr said, "while we would have proclaimed your death as the most infamous act of Ali."

And so saying, he left Aisha with the question that would surely unsettle her for the rest of her life. Where she had always thought of herself as the virtual queen of Islam, had she been all along merely a pawn in someone else's game?

Muawiya made the formal announcement of his son, Yazid, as his successor. He included no mention of Hussein, doubtless certain that he could persuade Ali's younger son into passivity just as he had done the elder. Since the father had accepted arbitration, and the older brother abdication, why should the younger brother behave any differently? Indeed, for another ten years, so long as Muawiya ruled, he would not. Hussein also knew how to be patient. Age, after all, was the one thing Muawiya could not control.

The gout and obesity caused by a lifetime of indulgence finally caught up with the fifth Caliph, though even in his last days, he made sure to present the image of someone in firm control. Propped up on pillows, he had *kohl* applied around his eyes to make them livelier and his face oiled to make it shine as though with vigor. But if vanity ruled the end of his life, so too did a sudden burst of piety. He instructed that he be buried in a shirt he said had been given him by Muhammad himself, a shirt he had kept along with some of the Prophet's nail clippings. "Cut up and grind these nail parings," he said, "then sprinkle them in my eyes and in my mouth. Thus God might have mercy on me by their blessing."

He died with Yazid by his side and Hussein on his mind. His last words to his son included a caution: "Hussein is a weak and insignificant man, but the people of Iraq will not leave him alone until they make him rebel. If that happens and you defeat him, pardon him, for he has close kinship to the Prophet and a great claim."

If Yazid had only heeded him, centuries of strife and division could perhaps have been avoided. But one way or another, history is often made by the heedless.

On April 22 in the year 680, Yazid was acclaimed Caliph. He

moved swiftly to consolidate his position, reconfirming Ziyad's son Ubaydallah as governor of Iraq in the hope of squelching any incipient uprising there. At the same time, he ordered his governor in Medina to arrest Hussein. "Act so fiercely that he has no chance to do anything before giving public allegiance to me," he wrote. "If he refuses, execute him."

But the same governor who had done Muawiya's bidding was not so quick to obey Yazid's orders. To prevent Hasan from being buried alongside Muhammad was one thing, but to kill Hussein, Muhammad's one remaining grandson? That was beyond the pale. "I could not do this, not for all the wealth and power in the world," he said.

Perhaps it was the governor himself who warned Hussein of what was afoot, or perhaps someone in his employ. All we know is that later that night, under cover of darkness, Hussein gathered together all his blood kin and fled the two hundred and fifty miles from Medina to Mecca.

That was when they began to arrive, messenger after messenger, exhausted from the long, urgent ride from Kufa. All of them bore letters begging Hussein to come to Iraq. Pleading with him to save them from the brutality and injustice of Yazid and his governor Ubaydallah. Calling on him to reclaim the caliphate and restore the soul of Islam. And then came the most persuasive letter of all, the one from Muslim, Hussein's cousin, assuring him that he had twelve thousand men ready to rise up under his leadership.

Hussein's response was to engrave the tragic rift between Shia and Sunni deep into the Muslim psyche. The third Imam, son of the first and brother of the second, set out from Mecca for Iraq in September of 680, with his family and just seventy-two armed men, not knowing that he was journeying toward his death—that within the month, he was destined to become forever the Prince of Martyrs.

chapter 13

It is not true that Hussein did not know what awaited him, the Shia maintain. The whole point is that he knew, yet set out nonetheless in full awareness of the sacrifice he would make. He had to have known, after all. There were so many warnings from so many people, warnings that began even before he started on the journey to Iraq with his family and those seventy-two warriors.

"Who can tell if the Kufans will really rise up and overthrow their oppressors?" worried one of his cousins. "These are people who can always be bought. They are slaves to the dirham. I fear they will desert you, even make war on you. "

Hussein seemed immune to such concerns. "By God, cousin, I know your advice is good and reasonable," he replied. "But what is fated is fated, and will happen whether I heed you or not."

Still, why court fate? Why ride toward it even as the warnings multiplied? Just one day's journey out of Mecca, a rider came with a message from another cousin. "I ask you by God to return," he wrote. "The hearts of the Iraqis may be with you, but I fear their swords belong to Yazid." Hussein merely registered the warning and kept going.

The following day brought a message from none other than the governor of Mecca. Risking his position, even his life, he gave Hussein his personal guarantee of "safe conduct, kindness, generosity, and protection" if he would only return to Mecca. But all Hussein would say in response was: "The best guarantee of safe conduct is that of God."

Besides, his numbers were growing. As his small caravan crossed over the jagged Hijaz mountains and into the high desert steppeland of northern Arabia, their pace timed to arrive at least every other night at a watering place—a well or at least a small shallow spring—word of their journey preceded them. Tribal warriors joined their ranks, roused by the idea of Hussein's reclaiming power for Arabia. By the end of the first week of the three-week journey, the original seventy-two warriors had swelled to several hundred. By the time they reached Iraq they would surely be an army.

Yet still the messages kept coming, each one a warning to beware of Iraq. Each time Hussein acknowledged it as "good and reasonable advice," and each time he ignored it. And then came the message that was surely impossible to ignore.

The messenger rode so hard that even in the twilight they could see the cloud of dust thrown up by his horse when he was still miles away. He came not from behind them, as the others had done, but from ahead—not from Mecca, that is, but from Iraq. They had just begun to set up camp when he pulled in, dismounted, and refused even a drink of water, so urgent was his news.

He had been sent by Hussein's cousin Muslim, who had not misled Hussein when he had written that he should set out immediately for Kufa. All the men of that city had indeed streamed out to pledge allegiance to Hussein as the true Caliph. They had indeed sworn to rise up and oust Yazid's governor Ubaydallah, and had called for Hussein to come and lead them on to Damascus, to unseat the usurper Yazid and to declare himself as the one and only true successor to his grandfather Muhammad and his father, Ali. All this was true, said the messenger, but things had changed.

If Muslim had been less devoted, he might perhaps have been a more careful judge of oaths given with such demonstrative alacrity. He might have remembered that oaths were one thing, the courage to follow through on them another. But he too had been caught up in the moment and had believed what he wanted to believe.

The men of Kufa could not be blamed. They had been carried away with hope, caught up in the heady idea of Hussein ready to overthrow oppression and injustice. But hope can be as evanescent as it is inspirational. The Kufans had families to care for, livings to make, lives to protect. They could recognize a superior force when they saw it.

Their governor, the son of the infamous Ziyad, was about to become still more infamous himself. Like his father before him—like any tyrannical ruler at any time, in fact—Ubaydallah knew how dangerous hope can be, and knew equally well how to quash it. There was no question of his ever allowing Hussein to reach Kufa, none either of Muslim's ever leaving the city alive.

"Do not expose yourselves to death," he told the Kufans. "If you shelter this man, you will taste the evil you have earned." And with the stick well established, he introduced the carrot: a large bounty on Muslim's head.

Nobody in Kufa entertained the slightest doubt as to exactly how Ubaydallah might wield the stick. Those who had displeased him in the past had been crucified in the camel market, their bodies left there to rot as their homes were demolished and their families turned out into the desert. The twelve thousand men who had so loudly and bravely pledged to fight alongside Muslim under Hussein's command were quickly reduced to only four thousand, then to three hundred, then to a mere handful. Within the space of a single day, Muslim found himself alone.

He had gone from house to house, knocking on barred doors and pleading for shelter from Ubaydallah's police. He never thought to be suspicious when one door opened at last, never imagined that this family had taken him in only in order to betray him and claim the bounty on his head.

When Ubaydallah's agents came for him that evening, he managed to persuade one brave soul to ride out of Kufa as fast as he could, both night and day, and intercept Hussein. "Tell him to turn back," Muslim said. "Tell him the Kufans have lied to me and lied to him."

The messenger had set out even as Muslim was being taken in chains to the governor's mansion. There was no doubt what Muslim's fate would be. It was the evening of Monday, September 8, in the year 680, and whatever hope there had been for an uprising was utterly extinguished. At dawn the following morning, at the exact time that Hussein and his small caravan set out from Mecca en route to Iraq, Muslim's headless body would be dragged to the camel market and strung up for all to see.

This was the story the messenger told, and before he had even finished, the tribal warriors began to melt away into the darkness, leaving only Hussein, his family, and the original seventy-two warriors. Hussein's mission had surely failed before it had even begun. Yet if he considered for a moment turning back, there is no record of it.

"Man journeys in darkness, and his destiny journeys toward him," he said, and traveled on.

Nobody disputes what happened. What is in dispute is why it happened. And that question hinges on the unknowable—on what Hussein was thinking.

Why did he continue when he knew that his cause was already lost? Was he so convinced of the rightness of his claim that he could no longer judge reality? So full of *nasb*—that inborn quality of nobility and honor—that he could not imagine anything but triumph for the righteousness of his cause? So high-minded that he was, in the end, merely naive? Did he act in desperation or out of the purest of motives? In sheer folly or in supreme wisdom?

He was not a warrior or a statesman. He was a revered scholar, honored since his brother's death as the one who more than any man alive embodied the spirit of Muhammad, and he was no longer a young man. Why not be content to live out his days in the peace and quiet of Mecca or Medina? Why not leave the business of politics and power to those who could handle it? And why place his fate in the hands of the Kufans, the people who not twenty years before had refused his father's call to arms against Muawiya? They had knuckled under first to Muawiya and his governor Ziyad, and now to Yazid and his governor Ubaydallah. Did Hussein really think they had changed? Did he imagine that right and justice could prevail over power and strength? That seventy-two warriors could take on the whole might of Yazid's army?

To Sunnis, Hussein's determination to travel on to Iraq would be the proof of his unsuitability to take the helm of a vast empire. They would call it a quixotic and ill-fated quest, one that should never have been undertaken. Hussein should have acknowledged reality, they say, and bowed to history.

In time they would cite the bitterly anti-Shia thirteenth-century scholar Ibn Taymiya, whose writings are still central to mainstream Sunni thought. Sixty years with an unjust leader were preferable to a single night with an ineffective one, Ibn Taymiya declared. His reasoning was that without an effectively run state, the implementation of Islamic law was impossible. But he was also clearly stating that church and state, as it were, were no longer one and the same, as they had been in Muhammad's time.

It was Ibn Taymiya who dubbed the first four Caliphs—Abu Bakr, Omar, Othman, and Ali—the *rashidun*, or rightly guided ones, and they are still known as such in Sunni Islam. The Caliphs who came after them were thus not rightly or divinely guided, no matter the lip service they gave to Islam or the grandiose titles they claimed like the "Shadow of God on Earth." But even those who lacked true spiritual authority could serve in other ways. Muawiya had prevented what had seemed the inevitable disintegration of the vast Islamic empire; if not for him, Islam might never have been able to survive. His son, Yazid, may have utterly lacked his father's political skill, but so long as he did not try to assume religious authority—something he had no interest in doing—his rule was to be considered tolerable. Spiritual guidance was not to be expected of political leaders, Ibn Taymiya was saying, and in this he was defending his own turf. A whole new religious establishment had come into being under the Umayyads and their Abbasid successors—the clerics and theologians known as the *ulama*—and as the empire's central political authority waned, they became the gatekeepers of Islam, much as the rabbis were the gatekeepers of Judaism through the centuries. The very idea of Hussein's acting out of spiritual authority and divine guidance was thus anathema to Ibn Taymiya and his ideological heirs.

But to the Shia, Hussein's journey to Iraq came to be the ultimate act of courage, the most noble self-sacrifice, made in a state of higher consciousness and with full knowledge of its import. Hussein would take the only way left him to expose the corruption and venality of the Umayyad regime, they would say. He would shock all Muslims out of their complacency and call them back to the true path of Islam through the leadership the Prophet had always intended, that of the *Ahl al-Bayt*. Divinely guided, he would sacrifice himself with the same purity of intention as the prophet Jesus did six hundred years before—a sacred sacrifice, willingly accepted for the sake of others. His surrender to death would be the ultimate act of redemption.

Hussein's story was about to become the foundation story of Shiism, its sacred touchstone, its Passion story. The long journey from Mecca to Iraq was his Gethsemane. Knowing that the Kufans had betrayed him, he rode on nonetheless, in full awareness of what was waiting for him.

Three weeks after leaving Mecca, his small caravan was within twenty miles of Kufa. They halted for the night at Qadisiya, the site of Omar's pivotal battle against the Persian army. That glorious victory now seemed to belong to another era, though it had been only forty-three years before. There would be no pivotal battle here this time. Ubaydallah had sent cavalry detachments from Kufa to block all the routes leading to the city, including the one from Qadisiya. His orders were to bring Hussein to him in chains to swear allegiance to Yazid.

But there would be no chains yet. Not even Ubaydallah could terrorize everyone. The captain of the hundred-man detachment that stopped Hussein was called Hurr—"freeborn" or "free man"—and as though living up to his name, he could not conceive of using force against the Prophet's grandson and his family. Instead, in a gesture of peaceful intent, he approached Hussein with his shield reversed. Then, like so many before him, he tried to persuade him that if he could not pledge allegiance to Yazid, he should at least turn back to Mecca.

"No, by God," came the answer. "I will neither give my hand like a humiliated man nor flee like a slave. May I not be called Yazid. Let me never accept humiliation over dignity." And in demonstration of that dignity, Hussein stood high in his saddle and addressed Hurr's men, many of them the same Kufans who had previously pledged to rise up against Yazid under his leadership.

"I have here two saddlebags full of your letters to me," he said. "Your messengers brought me your oath of allegiance, and if you now fulfill that oath, you will be rightly guided. My life will be with your lives, my family with your families. But if you break your covenant with me, you have mistaken your fortune and lost your destiny, for whoever violates his word, violates his own soul."

With men such as Yazid and his governor Ubaydallah in power, he said, "the goodness of the world is in retreat, and what was good is now bitter. Can you not see that truth is no longer practiced? That falsehood is no longer resisted? When that is so, I can only see life with such oppressors as tribulation, and death as martyrdom."

And there it was, out in the open: martyrdom—*shahadat*—the destiny toward which Hussein had been journeying, and that had been journeying toward him.

Shahadat is a word of subtle shadings, though as with the double meaning of *jihad,* this may be hard to see when the image of Islamic martyrdom is that of suicide bombers so blinded by righteousness that they sacrifice not just their own lives but all sense of humanity. In fact, while *shahadat* certainly means "self-sacrifice," it also means "acting as a witness," a double meaning that originally existed in English too, since the word "martyr" comes from the Greek for witness. This is why the Islamic declaration of faith—the equivalent of the *Shema Israel* or the Lord's Prayer—is called the *shahada,* the "testifying." And it is this dual role of martyr and witness that would inspire the leading intellectual architect of the Iranian Revolution of 1979 to utterly redefine Hussein's death as an act of liberation.

Ali Shariati is all but unknown in the West, yet for years he was idolized in Iran on a par with the Ayatollah Khomeini. He was not a cleric but a sociology professor well versed in theology. Educated at the Sorbonne, he was widely read in Western philosophy and literature and had translated both Sartre and Fanon into Persian, as well as Che Guevara. His blending of sociology and theology was to create a new kind of Islamic humanism that inspired millions, not the least because he was an absolutely charismatic speaker. By the early 1970s he was drawing crowds of thousands at a time—so many that they blocked the streets around his lecture hall in Teheran, listening in rapt silence to his voice on loudspeakers—and his published lectures had become Iran's all-time best sellers. Students and laborers, religious and secular, male and female—all those who would soon take to the streets to oust the Shah's regime—responded with an intense sense of hope and power as Shariati almost single-handedly gave new life to the core event of Shia Islam.

In one of his most famed lectures, he celebrated Hussein as the purest example of martyrdom. By refusing either to cooperate or to be pressured into silence, and by accepting that this would mean his own death, Hussein achieved nothing less than "a revolution in consciousness," one that far surpassed the details of its historical place and time to become "an eternal and transcendent phenomenon." And as Shariati went on to take his listeners into the seventh century, inside Hussein's mind, he had no need to stress the parallel with what they themselves faced under the repressive regime of the Shah.

"There is nothing left for Hussein to inherit," he said. "No army, no weapons, no wealth, no power, no force, not even an organized following. Nothing at all. The Umayyads occupy every base of society. The power of the tyrant, enforced with the sword or with money or with deception, brings a pall of stifled silence over everyone. All power is in the hand of the oppressive ruler. Values are determined solely by the regime. Ideas and thoughts are controlled by agents of the regime. Brains are washed, filled, and poisoned with falsehood presented in the name of religion, and if none of this works, faith is cut off with the sword. It is this power which Hussein must now face.

"This is the man who embodies all the values that have been destroyed, the symbol of all the ideals that have been abandoned. He appears with empty hands. He has nothing. The Imam Hussein now stands between two inabilities. He cannot remain silent, but neither can he fight. He has only one weapon, and that is death. If he cannot defeat the enemy, he can at least disgrace them with his own death. If he cannot conquer the ruling power, he can at least condemn it. For him, martyrdom is not a loss, but a choice. He will sacrifice himself on the threshold of the temple of freedom, and be victorious."

As Shariati spoke, *shahadat* became not just an act of witnessing but an act of revelation, exposing repression and oppression, corruption and tyranny. Hussein's martyrdom was no longer an end but a beginning. It was a call to action in the here and now.

"Martyrdom has a unique radiance," Shariati declared. "It creates light and heat in the world. It creates movement, vision, and hope. By his death, the martyr condemns the oppressor and provides commitment for the oppressed. In the iced-over hearts of a people, he bestows the blood of life and resurrection."

Such sacrifice was not for Islam alone. It was for all people, everywhere. Hussein acted as witness "for all the oppressed people of history. He has declared his presence in all wars, struggles, and battlefields for freedom of every time and land. He died at Karbala so that he may be resurrected in all generations and all ages."

Shariati was only forty-four when he himself died in 1977, two years before many of his students would be shot as they marched through the streets to oust the Shah. The cause of death was a heart attack, just three weeks after he had fled into exile in England. Some say it was brought on by the lingering effects of repeated arrest and interrogation by the Shah's security forces; others, that it was the result of poison covertly administered by secret agents—a swift, sharp jab from a hypodermic needle, perhaps, and the poison as sure as the ones developed by Muawiya's physician Ibn Uthal fourteen centuries earlier. Either way, the Shah was too late. Shariati had already transformed Hussein and his death at Karbala into the incandescent impetus for revolution.

For centuries, Hussein's martyrdom had been the central paradigm of Shia Islam, the symbol of the eternal battle between good and evil, but Shariati raised it to the level of liberation theology. He transformed Ashura, the ten-day commemoration of what happened at Karbala, taking it out of the realm of grief and mourning and into that of hope and activism. Karbala would no longer merely explain repression; it would be the inspiration to rise up against it, and Shariati's most famous call to action would become the new rallying cry of activist Shiism, chanted by idealistic young revolutionaries in the streets of Teheran even as the Shah's troops fired volley after volley into the crowd: "Every day is Ashura, and every land is Karbala."

If Hussein had resolved on martyrdom, Hurr was equally resolved not to be the one who brought it about. But he was confronted with a terrible dilemma: his orders from Ubaydallah on the one hand, his respect for Hussein on the other. This was the last surviving member of the People of the Cloak, the Prophet's own grandson, his flesh and blood. If Hurr could not allow him to continue on to Kufa, neither could he attack him.

It was Hussein himself who resolved Hurr's dilemma by turning in the least expected direction—not back to Arabia, or on to Kufa, but to the north. He led his small caravan along the desert bluff overlooking the immense flat valley formed by the Euphrates and the Tigris, and Hurr and his men rode alongside, more like an escort than an enemy detachment. At dusk, with the women and children tired and thirsty, Hussein gave the order to pitch their tents just below the bluff, within sight of fields and orchards watered by a branch of the Euphrates. It was Wednesday, the first day of the month of Muharram, and Hussein had reached his destination. He would travel no farther.

Two mornings later, the third day of Muharram, the small encampment had been surrounded by an army. When news reached Ubaydallah that Hurr had allowed Hussein to travel north instead of arresting him, he had sent no fewer than four thousand cavalry and archers out from Kufa, under the command of a notoriously ruthless general. If Hurr could not do the job, this man would.

His name was Shimr, a name destined to live on in the Shia annals of infamy alongside Muawiya, Yazid, and Ubaydallah. His orders were clear. He was to place Hussein's encampment under siege, cutting it off from all access to the river. In the terrible, stifling heat, he was to allow not one drop of water through his lines. Thirst would bring Hussein to his knees.

With four thousand trained soldiers against a mere seventy-two warriors, there was to be no escape. Nor did Hussein want any. Now that he had reached his final destination, he and all those with him would pass from the time-bound realm of history to the timeless one of heroes and saints.

As both the survivors and the besiegers told their memories of the next seven days, they would unfold as an almost stately series of events, as though the story were playing itself out on a stage far larger than this desolate patch of sand and stone. Even as they spoke, the tellers seemed aware of how sacred it would be, of how history would loose the bonds of gravity and soar into legend. While Shimr and his four thousand men waited for thirst to do its work, limiting themselves to occasional skirmishes with Hussein's warriors, undying memories were created. One by one, the iconic images of Shiism were brought into being.

There was Hussein's nephew Qasim, who married his cousin, Hussein's daughter, in that beleaguered encampment. Even as they all knew what was to come, they celebrated life over death, the future over the present. But the marriage was never consummated. No sooner was the ceremony over than Qasim demanded that he be allowed to go out to engage the enemy in single combat. It was his wedding day; he was not to be denied. Still in his embroidered wedding tunic, he stepped out from the tents toward Shimr's lines.

"There were ten of us in that sector, all on horseback," one of Shmir's men remembered, "and a young man all in white came toward us, a sword in his hand. Our horses were circling and prancing, and he was nervous, turning his head this way and that. I saw two pearls swinging from his ears as he moved." They did not swing long. The newly made groom was cut down, and all the promise of a wedding day abruptly snuffed out.

Then there was Abbas, Hussein's half brother, who wore two

white egret's plumes atop his chain mail helmet, a distinction awarded only the bravest warrior. Driven by the parched cries of the children as the small encampment ran out of water, he made his way through the enemy lines at night and filled a goatskin at the river, only to be ambushed on the way back. One man against many, he fought until his sword arm was cut off. At that, they say, he laughed, even as the blood poured out from him—"This is why God gave us two arms," he declared—and went on fighting with the other arm, the neck of the goatskin clenched between his teeth. But when the other arm too was cut off, all the valor in the world could not save him. The sword that pierced his heart also pierced the goatskin, and the water ran red with his blood as it spilled out onto the sandy soil.

And there was Hussein's eldest son, Ali Akbar. He was on the brink of adulthood, a fresh-faced youth, yet he too insisted on going out to do single combat, determined to die fighting rather than of thirst. "A lad came out against us with a face like the first splinter of the moon," said one of those who crowded in on him. "One of his sandals had a broken strap, though I can't remember if it was the left one or the right. The left, I think."

When Ali Akbar was quickly cut down, Hussein "swooped down like a hawk" to cradle his dying son. That is how the two are still shown in Shia posters, a famed pose deliberately mirrored in other posters showing Muqtada al-Sadr, the leader of the Mahdi Army, cradling the body of his father, the revered cleric Muhammad Sadiq al-Sadr, who, along with his two older sons, was murdered by Saddam's thugs in 1998.

But perhaps the most iconic image of all was that of Hussein's infant son. Just three months old, he was so weak from dehydration that he could no longer even cry. Hussein himself, despairing, came out in front of the tents and held the infant up in his arms for all the enemy to see. His voice cracked and parched with thirst, he begged Shimr's men to have mercy on these children, to allow water at least for them.

The only reply was an arrow, shot straight into the neck of the infant even as he lay in Hussein's outstretched hands.

They say that the infant's blood poured between Hussein's fingers onto the ground and that as it did so, he called on God for vengeance. But stories told again and again, through the generations, develop their own logic. In time it was said that Hussein beseeched God not for vengeance but for mercy. "Oh God, be my witness, and accept this sacrifice!" he said, and the infant's blood flew upward from his hands in defiance of gravity and never returned to earth.

Then came the eve of the final day—*ashura*, the tenth of Muharram—the setting for the Shia equivalent of the Last Supper. Hussein begged those of his men who still survived to leave him to his fate. "All of you, I hereby absolve you from your oath of allegiance to me, and place no obligation upon you. Go home now, under cover of darkness. Use the night as a camel to ride away upon. These men of Yazid's want only me. If they have me, they will stop searching for anyone else. I beg you, leave for your homes and your families."

They stayed. Their mouths parched, lips swollen, voices harsh and rasping with thirst, they swore never to leave him. "We will fight with you until you reach your destination," one of them proclaimed. And another: "By God, if I knew that I was to be burned alive and my ashes scattered, and then revived to have it done to me again a thousand times, I still would never leave you. How then could I leave when what I now face is a matter of dying only once?"

"Then call upon God and seek his forgiveness," said Hussein, "for our final day will come tomorrow." And then he used the Islamic phrase uttered in the face of death: "We belong to God, and to God we shall return."

It was a long night, that last night. A night of prayer and preparation. Hussein took off his chain mail and put on a simple white seamless robe—a shroud. He had myrrh melted in a bowl and anointed himself and his men with the perfume, and all of them knew that they were being anointed as corpses are, for death.

"Tears choked me and I pushed them back," one of Hussein's daughters would remember. "I kept silent and knew that the final tribulation had come upon us."

Tears are infectious, almost physically so. Whether in a movie house or in real life, people fight back tears of sympathy and then find that their vision has blurred and the fight has already been lost.

But for the Shia, there is no fighting back tears. On the contrary, they are encouraged. Grief and sorrow are the signs of deep faith, the overt expression not only of atonement and horror but of an abiding conviction that the tears count, that they have purpose.

In the ten days leading up to Ashura, every detail of the ordeal at Karbala fourteen hundred years ago is recalled and reenacted. The story so central to Shia Islam has been kept alive year after year, century after century, not in holy writ but by the impassioned force of memory, of repetition and reenactment.

A vast cycle of *taziya*, or Passion plays, is staged every year—so many of them in so many places that the Oberammergau cycle of medieval Christianity is a pale mirror by comparison. The pacing is almost stately, the dialogue more a series of speeches than give-and-take, but no Broadway or West End performance has ever had so rapt an audience. Every appearance onstage of a black-robed Yazid or Ubaydallah or Shimr is greeted by hisses and boos. The newlywed groom about to bid farewell to his still-virgin bride before going to his death is acclaimed with tears. As Hussein holds up his infant son in front of the enemy, people beat their breasts and wail softly, almost to themselves, as though if they could stifle their sobs, the tragedy would somehow be averted.

But the height of the Passion plays, the most intense point, comes not when Hussein is actually killed but at the moment he dons his white shroud. For all the terrible pathos of what has already happened, this moment—one of the least dramatic to Western eyes—is the most unbearable for the audience. It is the moment of calm in the face of death, the willing acceptance of the call to self-sacrifice.

For ten days the commemoration of Ashura has been leading to this moment. Men have gathered in *husseiniya*—"Hussein houses"—special halls set aside specifically for telling the story of Karbala, for tears and reflection, grief and meditation. Women have crowded into one another's homes to build the wedding canopy for Hussein's daughter and his nephew Qasim, then decorate it with silk ribbons and strew petals on the floor, creating a marriage bed for the union that will never be consummated. They stretch another, smaller canopy over a cradle and fill it with offerings for Hussein's infant son: candies and toys. They implore Hussein to intercede for them and for their children in their twenty-first-century lives, to keep them safe from drugs and violence and any of life's other temptations and dangers. And they mourn, beating their breasts and slapping their cheeks faster and faster as their chanting picks up its pace—"Hussein, Hussein, Hussein, Hussein, Hussein"—until they have no strength left.

Everything culminates on the tenth day, the day of the processions. Men and boys march by the hundreds in the villages, by the thousands and tens of thousands in the cities. Whole squadrons of men beat their chests in unison, their hands clenched into hollow fists, the better to reverberate against the rib cage. And with each step, each blow, "Oh Hussein, oh Hussein . . ."

The echoing thud of one man striking himself this way is sobering; the sound of thousands can be heard miles away, as loud as the tolling of a cathedral bell at Easter, and far more terrifying for the knowledge that this is the sound of flesh on flesh.

Some go further. They beat themselves not with their fists but with flails of chains, and at the end of each length of chain, a small blade. They flick the flails over the left shoulder, then over the right, again and again until their backs are bloodied. A few even use knives to slash at their foreheads so that the copious blood of a head wound flows down over their faces to mix with their tears. The sight fills even the most resolute onlooker with awe and a kind of sacred horror.

Throughout the procession, people carry posters blown up large, garlanded with flowers and with green and black silk banners—green for Islam, black for mourning. Some are the standard ones of Hussein, his *keffiya* falling in graceful folds to his shoulders, but others are specifically for Ashura. These show his bare head angled back, blood on his forehead and his mouth open in agony. The head seems to float in space, and in a way it does: it is speared on the point of a lance.

And at the center of each procession, a white riderless horse, Hussein's horse, its saddle empty.

The sun rose inexorably on the morning of the tenth of Muharram, October 10, in the year 680. As it gained height and heat, the last of the seventy-two warriors in Hussein's encampment went out one by one to meet their deaths. By the time the sun was high in the sky, only Hussein himself remained.

He said farewell to the women of his family, mounted his white stallion—Lahik, the Pursuer, he was called—and rode out from the tents to confront his destiny. As he charged into the enemy lines, the archers fired, volley after volley. Arrows studded the horse's flanks, yet still he kept charging. Astride him, Hussein struck out left and right with his sword and for a few moments, it hardly seemed to matter that he was only one man against four thousand. "By God I have never seen his like before or since," one of Shimr's men would remember. "The foot soldiers retreated from him as goats retreat from an advancing wolf."

But it could not last. "Why are you waiting?" Shimr yelled at his troops. "You sons of men who urinate at both ends! Kill him, or may your mothers be bereaved of you!" An arrow struck home in Hussein's shoulder, the force of it throwing him to the ground, and they finally crowded in on him.

By the time they were done, there were thirty-three knife and sword wounds on his body. Even that was not enough. As though trying to hide the evidence, they spurred their horses over his corpse again and again, trampling the grandson of the Prophet, the last of the five People of the Cloak, into the dust of Karbala.

At that moment, what the Sunnis consider history became sacred history for the Shia, and the aura of sacredness would permeate the memories of what happened next. There is no mention in the earliest accounts of Hussein's three-year-old daughter Sukayna roaming the battlefield; no mention either of tears streaming from the eyes of his white horse or of the sudden appearance of two white doves. But who can hold that against the millions of Shia for whom Ashura is what defines them? Details accrue around a story of such depth and magnitude, in the Passion of Hussein as in the Passion of Christ.

Eventually, those who remembered would tell how Lahik, that noblest of all Arab stallions, bowed down and dipped his forehead in his master's blood, then went back to the women's tent, tears streaming from his eyes, and beat his head on the ground in mourning. They would tell how two doves flew down and dipped their wings in Hussein's blood, then flew south, first to Medina and then to Mecca, so that when people there saw them, they knew what had happened, and the wailing of grief began. They would tell how the three-year-old Sukayna wandered out onto the battlefield in search of her father, crying out for him piteously, surrounded by blood-soaked corpses.

With time, it made no difference if Abbas had really fought on with only one arm, or if the horse really did cry, or if the doves really did fly down as though from heaven. Faith and need said they did. The stories have become as true as the most incontrovertible fact, if not more so, because they have such depth of meaning. As with the death of Christ, the death of Hussein soars beyond history into metahistory. It enters the realm of faith and inspiration, of passion both emotional and religious.

Shimr's men hacked off Hussein's head, along with those of all seventy-two of his warriors. They slung most of the severed heads in sacks across their horses' necks, each one proof of the kill, a guarantee of a cash reward from Ubaydallah back in Kufa. But Hussein's head was singled out. Shimr ordered it speared on a lance and carried like a trophy in front of his army. As the Quran had been desecrated at Siffin, so now was Hussein's head at Karbala.

Shimr did not bury the seventy-two headless corpses; instead, he ordered them left behind in the desert for hyenas and wolves to feed on. He had the women and children put in chains and led them on the long trek to Kufa, stumbling behind the head of Hussein. When they reached the governor's palace, Ubaydallah laughed with pleasure as Shimr tossed the severed trophy onto the floor in front of him. He even poked at the head with his cane, sending it rolling over the stone tiles. At the sight, one elderly companion of the Prophet was so appalled that he could contain himself no longer, no matter the danger. "Take your cane away, by God!" he erupted. "How often have I seen the Messenger of God kiss that face you now desecrate!" And in tears, the old man limped out of the assembly hall before the soldiers could stop him, to speak his mind one last time.

"A slave has given power to a slave and has made the people his inheritance," he told the people outside. "You, Arabs, are the slaves after today. You killed the son of Fatima when the bastard governor ordered you. You have accepted shame and humiliation. Let destruction come to those who accept humiliation."

The old man's anger and dismay struck deep into the collective conscience. The Prophet was dead not fifty years, yet here the men of his family had been massacred, and the women humiliated. As the news spread throughout Islam, a sense of bitter shame spread with it, and a new name came into being for the family of Muhammad: *Bayt al-Ahzan,* the House of Sorrow.

Yet this ignominious death in the desert, like that ignominious death on the cross six centuries earlier, would prove to be not the end but only the beginning.

chapter 14

WOLVES AND HYENAS DID NOT DEVOUR THE CORPSES AS SHIMR had planned. Once he had led away his captives, farmers ventured out from a nearby village, buried the seventy-two headless bodies, and marked the graves. Just four years later, pilgrims—the precursors of the millions who now arrive each year—began to arrive on the anniversary of the massacre, and it was they who named the gravesite Karbala, "the place of trial and tribulation."

Hussein's head would have many resting places, its presence spreading along with the story of what had happened. Most say it is buried by the east wall of the Grand Mosque in Damascus, but some have it in a shrine near the main entry to the Al-Azhar Mosque in Cairo, while yet others maintain that it was spirited away to Azerbaijan for safekeeping. Some even say it was returned to Karbala. But far more important than the physical remains, what survived was the story, and it was the survivors who told it—the women and the girls, and one boy.

Ali Zayn al-Abidin, Hussein's adolescent son, never took part in the fighting. He could not rise from his bedding in the women's tent.

Struck by severe fever, he had tossed and turned helplessly as his friends, his kin, and finally his father went out to meet their deaths. So when Shimr and his men came bursting into the women's tent and caught sight of him, the sick boy was an easy and obvious target, and he too would certainly have been killed were it not for his aunt, Hussein's sister Zaynab.

"Do not let Satan take away your courage," Hussein had told her on that final night, and now she displayed that courage. She hurled herself over her nephew and defied Shimr to run her through with his sword. "If you kill him, then you kill me with him," she declared.

Not even Shimr, it seemed, could kill the granddaughter of the Prophet in cold blood. Instead, he gave the order to take the boy captive along with the women. But Zaynab would do more than keep alive Hussein's one remaining son; she would keep alive the memory of Karbala itself. Her words of grief as she was being led away in chains, her clothing torn and head bare, would haunt Islam through the centuries.

"Oh Muhammad, Muhammad, may the angels of heaven bless you!" she wailed. "Here is Hussein in the open, stained with blood and his limbs torn off. Oh Muhammad! Your daughters are prisoners, your progeny are killed, and the east wind blows dust over them."

Nobody in Iraq needed to be told what that east wind brought with it. That was the wind of blinding dust storms, the very breath of trial and tribulation.

Even Shimr's men repented when they heard her, or so at least some of them would claim. "By God, she made every friend and every foe weep," one said later. But if the soldiers did indeed weep, they still obeyed orders. Ubaydallah had the captives publicly humiliated by parading them through Kufa and, only once that was done, sent them on to the Caliph Yazid in Damascus, along with the severed heads.

Some say it was not Ubaydallah but Yazid himself who then

poked at Hussein's head with a cane and laughed gleefully as it rolled on the floor at his feet. But most say he angrily cursed Shimr and Ubaydallah for their "excess of zeal," his conscience roused by the fact that Zaynab was there to call him to account.

No matter the chains, the torn clothing, the dust and blisters of the long desert march from Kufa, she stood proudly in front of the Umayyad Caliph and publicly shamed him. "You, your father, and your grandfather submitted to the faith of my father, Ali, the faith of my brother Hussein, the faith of my grandfather Muhammad," she told him. "Yet you have vilified them unjustly and oppressed the very faith you profess."

At this, Yazid himself broke down in tears. "If I had been there, Hussein, you would not have been killed," he swore, and gave orders for the captives to be treated as honored guests in his own household. On the fortieth day after Karbala—the day the Shia commemorate as *Arbain*, or "forty"—he gave the women and girls and the one surviving son his assurance of protection and had them escorted back to Medina.

Perhaps he had remembered what some say was Muawiya's dying caution to him: "If you defeat Hussein, pardon him, for he has a great claim." If so, it was too late. Reviled by the Shia, Yazid would hardly be better treated in memory by the Sunnis. Few would grieve when he died only three years after Karbala, just as his forces were poised to take the city of Mecca, which had risen up in rebellion under the son of Aisha's ill-fated brother-in-law Zubayr. Fewer still would grieve when his sickly thirteen-year-old son died just six months after that. And it is probably safe to say that none grieved for his second cousin Marwan, who then proclaimed himself Caliph. The man who had played such a devious role behind the scenes throughout Othman's and Ali's caliphates finally achieved the power he had coveted for so long, but only briefly; within the year he would be smothered to death by his own wife.

All the while, "the Karbala factor," as it would come to be called, was rapidly gaining strength. The story told by the seventh-century survivors would not only endure but would grow in power to find renewed life in the twentieth century.

"Religion is an amazing phenomenon that plays contradictory roles in people's lives," said Ali Shariati, the charismatic lecturer who helped lay the intellectual foundation of the Iranian Revolution of 1979. "It can destroy or revitalize, put to sleep or awaken, enslave or emancipate, teach docility or teach revolt."

Khomeini understood him perfectly. Like Shariati, the Ayatollah grasped that Karbala was an enormously loaded symbol, a deep well of emotional, social, and political significance, seemingly infinitely adaptable to time and circumstance. Under the regime of the Shah, with political dissent banned under pain of imprisonment, torture, and execution, religion could become the umbrella language of protest and resistance. The Karbala story was the perfect vehicle for this. Its themes broke through the usual social and economic dividing lines to resonate with clerics and secular intellectuals, liberals and conservatives, urban Marxists and tradition-bound villagers alike.

"Let the blood-stained banners of Ashura be raised wherever possible as a sign of the coming day when the oppressed shall avenge themselves on the oppressors," Khomeini wrote from exile in France in November 1978, and on Ashura itself, which fell on December 11 that year, the traditional processions were transformed into a powerful political weapon. Under intense pressure, the Shah lifted martial law for just two days, and millions of Iranians responded to Khomeini's call and marched in the streets, alternating the ritual cry of "Death to Yazid!" with a new one: "Death to the Shah!"

Forty days later, on *Arbain*, Khomeini again called on the Karbala factor, comparing those killed in the streets by the Shah's troops with those killed by Yazid's troops fourteen hundred years earlier. "It is as if the blood of our martyrs were the continuation of the blood of the martyrs of Karbala," he wrote. "It is our religious and national duty to organize great marches on this day." Despite the reimposition of martial law, the Karbala story again became the means of mass mobilization, and again the Shah's troops opened fire, creating yet more martyrs. By the end of the month the Shah had fled into exile.

The revolution had succeeded, but with what many would see as a vengeance. Within two months the Islamic Republic was declared, and Khomeini announced himself the Supreme Leader. Liberal Muslims and secular intellectuals now discovered the other side of the religious fervor they had helped foment. Revolution gave way to theocracy; freedom and justice, to Islamic dictatorship. Thousands of secular and liberal activists who had helped bring about the revolution were imprisoned and executed. Women disappeared behind head-to-toe veils, and even the young chador-clad women who had toted submachine guns in the streets of Teheran, calling themselves "the commandos of Zaynab," were quickly assigned to more traditional duties. Many of Shariati's teachings were soon declared un-Islamic, and his image, once featured alongside Khomeini on everything from posters to postage stamps, disappeared from view.

The Karbala story was still used, though in a far more deliberately manipulative way. In the Iran-Iraq War of the 1980s, thousands of Iranian boys were given headbands inscribed with the word "Karbala," then sent off to become human minesweepers. Wave after wave of them ran headlong into Iraqi minefields to be blown up to clear the way for Iranian troops, each of them in the desperate faith that he was heading for a martyr's paradise. Frontline troops were inspired to sacrifice by visits from singers and chanters of Karbala lamentations, the most famed of whom was known as "Khomeini's Nightingale." Khomeini had swept into power with the help of the Karbala factor, then taken control of it, taming it into the docility and obedience Shariati had warned of.

But the newly proven power of Karbala was not to be so easily controlled in the country of its birth, Iraq, where it was soon to bind together not only the past and the present, but also the future.

Just one of Hussein's five sons had survived, but for the Shia, that one was enough. He would be the fourth of twelve Imams, the twelve seen on posters all over the Shia world, seated in a V formation behind Ali at their head. The imamate passed from father to son, each of them endowed with divine knowledge and grace. And after Karbala, each of them, the Shia believe, was poisoned, first by order of the Umayyad Caliphs, then by order of their successors, the Abbasids. Each, that is, except the last, the twelfth Imam, the one whose face is hidden in the posters. Where his face should be, there is just a patch of white, as though the radiance of sanctity would be too much for human eyes.

In fact the fourth, fifth, and sixth Imams—Hussein's one surviving son, his grandson, and his great-grandson Jaafar al-Sadiq, who laid the foundation of Shia theology—seem to have lived long lives in Medina. Whether poison did indeed account for their deaths is more a matter of faith than of record. But it is clear that once the Abbasids came to power, the life expectancy of the Shia Imams drastically decreased.

The Abbasids ousted the Umayyads just seventy years after Karbala and brought the caliphate back from Syria to Iraq. In 762 they built a magnificent new capital city on the banks of the Tigris. Laid out in a perfect circle, it was originally called Medinat as-Salaam—"City of Peace"—though it quickly became better known as Baghdad, from the Persian for "gift of paradise."

By the end of the eighth century, under the fabled Caliph Harun al-Rashid, the Muslim empire stretched all the way from Spain to India, and Baghdad had become the center of an extraordinary flowering in the arts and sciences. Mathematics reached a new level of sophistication; indeed, the word "algebra" comes from Arabic. Literary output soared, most notably with the famed *Thousand and One Nights*, which originated, as its stories put it, "in the time of Harun al-Rashid." Exhaustive histories, the ones on which this book is based, were compiled. But for the Shia, it all came at a high price.

The Abbasids had seized power with strong Shia support, since they claimed to be descendants of Muhammad's uncle Abbas. If not exactly *Ahl al-Bayt*, they presented themselves as at least very close. But once in power, they dropped the Shia banner, and the Shia reacted with a deep sense of betrayal—and with division on how to counter such betrayal. Those taking a more activist anti-Abbasid stand included the Zaydis, a Yemeni denomination, some of whom maintained that the imamate had ended with only seven Imams, and the Ismailis, who at first believed it had ended with five, and struck out for power in their own right. One Ismaili branch went on to found the Fatimid dynasty, build the city of Cairo, and rule Egypt from the tenth to the twelfth century, while another is still headed by the Aga Khan. But the vast majority of Shia would eventually hew to belief in twelve Imams and, following their example, focus more on religious devotion than on opposition to the Sunni Caliphs.

After Hussein, all the Imams steered clear of political involvement in favor of pure theology. But where it seemed that the Umayyads could afford to ignore them so long as they were safely distant in Medina, their existence posed more of a threat to the Abbasids. Their line of direct descent from Muhammad represented a clear contradiction of the Abbasid claim to leadership. The Imams, that is, were potential rallying points for resistance and rebellion. So whereas the Umayyads had apparently let them be in Medina, the Abbasids brought them close. In fact, from the seventh Imam on, each one was brought to Iraq and either imprisoned or kept under house arrest. And it seems quite likely that each one was indeed poisoned.

The gold-domed shrines so easily confused by Westerners are built over the tombs of the Imams. The shrines of Ali in Najaf and the twin shrines of Hussein and his half brother Abbas in Karbala draw the largest numbers of pilgrims, but the sanctity of the other shrines is almost as great. The Khadhimiya shrine in Baghdad contains the tombs of the seventh and ninth Imams; the Imam Reza shrine in the Iranian city of Mashhad is built over the tomb of the eighth Imam; and the tenth and eleventh Imams are entombed in the Askariya shrine in Samarra, on the Tigris River sixty miles north of Baghdad.

The name of the Askariya shrine encodes the fate of the two Imams buried there. It comes from the word for a military garrison or camp, and this is what Samarra was—the Pentagon, as it were, of the Abbasid dynasty. The tenth and eleventh Imams were kept under house arrest there, making them literally *askariya*, "the ones kept in camp."

But the Askariya shrine has even greater significance in Shiism, for the Samarra garrison is where the Shia say the twelfth Imam was born—the last and ultimate inheritor of the pure bloodline of Muhammad through Fatima and Ali, and the central messianic figure of mainstream Shiism.

His birthday is celebrated each year in what might be seen as the Shia equivalent of Christmas Eve, a joyful counterpoint to Ashura. "The Night of Wishes and Prayers," it is called, a night when homes are hung with balloons and strings of colored lights, when people drum and sing and dance, when confetti and candies are strewn in the streets and fireworks light up the sky. A night, it seems, when wishes and prayers really could come true, which is why on this night the Shia faithful make their way not to Samarra, where the twelfth Imam was born, but to Karbala, where it is believed he will return, followed by Hussein on one side and Jesus on the other.

The twelfth Imam's name is Muhammad al-Mahdi: "the one who guides divinely." He is often referred to by a host of other names, including Al-Qaim, "He Who Rises Up"; Sahib as-Zaman, "Lord of the

Ages"; and Al-Muntazar, the "Awaited One." Mostly, though, he is known simply as the Mahdi.

It is said that he was the sole child of a clandestine marriage between the eleventh Imam and a captive granddaughter of the Byzantine emperor, and that his birth was kept secret lest Abbasid poisons find him too. But on the death of his father in the year 872, when he was only five years old, a far more radical means of protection was needed, so it is the core tenet of mainstream Shia belief that in that year the Mahdi evaded the fate of his predecessors by descending into a cave beneath Samarra.

He did not die in that cave, but entered a state of *ghrayba*, "occultation," a strictly correct translation that is also perfect in the spiritual sense, since it comes from astronomy, where it refers to one planetary body's passing in front of another, hiding it from view. An eclipse of the sun or the moon is a matter of occultation, the source of light hidden and yet the light itself radiating out around the edges. But more plainly speaking, *ghrayba* means simply "concealment," which is why the Mahdi is often called the Hidden Imam.

This concealment is not permanent. It is a temporary state, a suspension of presence in the world rather than an absence, and it has lasted more than a thousand years so far. The Mahdi will reveal himself again only on the Day of Judgment, when he will return to herald a new era of peace, justice, and victory over evil.

The day and month of his return are known: the tenth of Muharram, the very day on which Hussein was killed at Karbala. But the year remains unknown. And precisely because it is unknown, it is always imminent, and never more so than in times of turmoil.

One much-quoted eleventh-century treatise lists the signs and portents leading up to the Mahdi's return, many of them familiar from Christian apocalyptic visions. Nature behaves in strange and ominous ways: lunar and solar eclipses within the same month, the sun rising in the west and then standing still, a star in the east as bright as the full moon, a black wind, earthquakes, locusts. But the chaos and disorder of nature are merely mirrors of chaos and disorder in human affairs.

The power of the nonbelievers will spread. Fire will drop from the sky and consume Kufa and Baghdad. False mahdis will rise up and wage bloody battles against one another. Muslims will take arms to throw off the reins of foreign occupation and regain control of their land. There will be a great conflict in which the whole of Syria will be destroyed.

All this and more can sound extraordinarily specific in the modern Middle East. Iranians threw off the reins of foreign control in the revolution of 1979–80, first taking hostage and then expelling the Americans who had shored up the Shah's regime. Fire dropped from the sky in the form of American bombardment of Baghdad during the 2003 invasion of Iraq, and false mahdis waged bloody sectarian battles against one another in the vacuum of power created by the invasion. The great conflict in Syria is easily seen as that against Israel, whose territory was once part of the Muslim province of Syria.

So when Khomeini took such a strong anti-American stance and framed his stranglehold on power by announcing that he was the representative of the Mahdi and thus carrying out the Mahdi's will, it was only a matter of time until rumors spread that he was in fact the Mahdi himself, returned to the world. There is no knowing how the rumors began—such is the nature of rumor—but it seems reasonable to suppose that they had some guidance from interested parties. Since Khomeini had already been hailed as "the heir of Hussein" and "the Hussein of our time," it was not such a great leap from the third to the twelfth Imam. Indeed, Khomeini would take the title Imam, as though he were the natural successor to the twelve, and though he never confirmed the rumors, he never quite denied them either. They subsided only with his death in 1989, when he was entombed in a gold-domed shrine clearly modeled on those of Ali and Hussein.

Messianic fervor also helped fuel the Iran-Iraq War of the 1980s, when Iranian troops at the front woke many nights to see a shrouded fig-ure on a white horse blessing them. Who else could it be, it was said, but the Mahdi himself? In the event, the mysterious figures turned out to be professional actors sent to create exactly that impression, but nobody could ever be sure if they appeared as a sincere homage or in cynical ma-nipulation of popular faith.

Certainly there was nothing cynical about the way Iranian presi-dent Mahmud Ahmadinejad invoked the Mahdi when he took office in 2005. He was utterly sincere, and this made what he said all the more dis-turbing. Government policy would be guided by the principle of hasten-ing the Mahdi's return, he said—an idea quite familiar to fundamentalist Christians trying to hasten the second coming of the Messiah, and to fundamentalist Jews trying to hasten the first. Ahmadinejad appeared to be tapping into a deep well of sincerely felt faith, both his own and that of others. But as he repeatedly used the symbolism of "hastening the re-turn" over the years, linking it to anti-American and anti-Israel rhetoric, many in the West worried about the apocalyptic implications, especially given Iran's nuclear ambitions.

In Iraq, the sense of apocalypse was closer to home as chaos fol-lowed the American invasion of 2003. The radical cleric Muqtada al-Sadr could not have chosen a more powerfully emotive name for his Mahdi Army. The name itself is a call to action that goes far beyond Muqtada's declared aims of freeing Iraq from American occupation and battling Sunni extremism, and he made this crystal clear when he an-nounced the formation of the social and political wing of his movement in 2008. It was to be called Mumahdiun, "those who prepare the way for the Mahdi."

But if faith can be used as a way to channel hope for the future, it can also be used against that hope. That was what happened in Feb-ruary 2006, when somebody—most likely the extremist Sunni group Al Qaida in Iraq—placed explosives throughout the Askariya Mosque in Samarra. The magnificent golden dome collapsed, setting off a vicious cycle of Shia reprisals and Sunni counterreprisals just when it seemed that the civil war was finally calming down—a cycle made yet worse when the two gold minarets that had survived the first bombing were blown up and destroyed the following year.

Al Qaida in Iraq could not have made a stronger statement. No Shia missed the significance of this wholesale destruction, for the Askariya Mosque contained not only the tombs of the tenth and eleventh Imams but also the shrine built over Bir al-Ghayba—the "Well of Disappearance"—the cave where the twelfth Imam had descended and disappeared from the world, to remain hidden until his return.

That cave was the real target of the attack. Attack the shrine of Hussein at Karbala, as has been done many times over the centuries, most notably in living memory by Saddam Hussein's troops, and you attack the heart of Shia Islam. Attack Ali's shrine in Najaf, as was done when American troops tried to oust the Mahdi Army from it in 2004, and you attack its soul. But attack the Askariya shrine in Samarra, and you commit something even worse: you attack the Mahdi and thus the core of Shia hope and identity. The destruction of the Askariya shrine was an attack not just on the past, or even the present, but on the future.

chapter 15

ATROCITIES LIKE THE ASHURA MASSACRE AT KARBALA IN 2004 and the destruction of the Askariya shrine in 2006 inevitably become the focus of news reports, serving as markers of escalating conflict. Imprinted as deep in the collective memory as the events of fourteen hundred years ago, they seem to ensure that the Karbala story is one without end, destined only to grow in power and significance with every new outrage.

But destiny is not so straightforwardly determined. Within a hundred years of Hussein's death at Karbala, the split between Sunni and Shia had begun to solidify, yet it did so more around theology than politics. The extraordinary range of ethnic differences in the vast empire meant that central political authority was hard to maintain; by the ninth century, as the Abbasid dynasty weakened, religious and political authority were well on the way to being separate spheres. In the lack of a political consensus, the *ulama*—religious scholars and clerics—created an Islamic one across ethnic lines and gained the status they still have today, when more than four out of five Muslims are non-Arab.

Separate Sunni and Shia collections of *hadith* were compiled, and the differences between them represented competing historical memories. They told different versions of the same stories, disagreeing not on what had taken place in the seventh century but on what it meant. Where Sunnis would see Muhammad's choice of Abu Bakr as his companion on the *hijra*—the emigration to Medina—as proof that he intended Abu Bakr to be his successor, for instance, the Shia would see his declaration at Ghadir Khumm as proof of his designation of Ali. The Sunnis, in effect, would honor history as it had taken shape; the Shia would honor it as they believe it should have taken shape, and as they maintain it indeed did in a realm other than the worldly one.

By the tenth century, the Sunni Abbasid Caliphs had been reduced to little more than figureheads. Political power was in the hands of the Buyids, a strongly pro-Shia group from northeastern Persia that instituted the Ashura rituals as we know them today. But Baghdad's hold on the empire continued to weaken, and by 1258 the city was helpless to resist the Mongol invasion under Hulagu, a grandson of Genghis Khan. The once-great empire split into a welter of localized dynasties, both Sunni and Shia. It would be another two centuries until relative stability was achieved, with the Middle East once more divided as it had been under the Byzantines and the Persians. This time the divide would be between the Sunni Ottoman empire based in Turkey and the powerful Safavid dynasty in Persia—today's Iran—which made Shiism the state religion. Again, Iraq was the borderland, the territory where the two sides met and clashed most violently.

Yet despite the horrendous eruptions of violence in Iraq—Karbala itself came under attack numerous times, most savagely by the Wahhabis in 1802 and by Turkish troops in 1843, when one-fifth of the city's population was slaughtered—Shia and Sunnis for the most part accepted difference rather than exacerbate it. On the everyday level, they sometimes even embraced it. The *ulama* would never be able to control popular religious customs that contradicted official practice. Veneration of Ali was common among Sunnis as well as Shia, and still is. Despite official Sunni abhorrence of "idolatry," pilgrimage to shrines and prayer for the intercession of holy men remained popular among Sunnis as well as Shia. And while Ashura commemorations sometimes sparked Sunni attacks, at other times Sunnis participated in the rituals along with their Shia neighbors. What happened was less a result of theological difference than of the politics of the time. As with any matter of faith, in modern America as much as in the Middle East of centuries ago, the Sunni-Shia split could always be manipulated for political advantage.

Whatever balance there was would be changed utterly by World War I and the consequent partitioning of the former Ottoman Empire. Western intervention reshaped the Middle East, often in what seems astonishingly cavalier fashion. The British enabled the Wahhabi-Saudi takeover of Arabia, installed a foreign Sunni king over Shia majority Iraq, and shored up the Nazi sympathizer Reza Khan as Shah of Iran. After World War II, the United States took over as prime mover. Motivated by Cold War ideology, it helped engineer a coup d'état against Iran's newly elected prime minister Muhammad Mossadegh and reinstated the autocratic regime of Reza Khan's son, Shah Reza Pahlavi, under whom Iran first aspired to nuclear power—with American encouragement. Successive U.S. administrations backed the Wahhabi-dominated kingdom of Saudi Arabia not only for access to its oil but also as a bulwark against Nasser's pro-Soviet regime across the Red Sea in Egypt. In the 1980s the United States joined forces with Saudi Arabia and Pakistan to fund the anti-Soviet *mujahidin*—literally *jihad* fighters, or as Ronald Reagan preferred to call them, freedom fighters—in Afghanistan, and in a rather stunning example of unintended consequences, these troops later formed the basis of the Taliban. In that same decade, the United States found itself arming both sides in the Iran-Iraq War, supporting Saddam Hussein in order to counter the fierce anti-Americanism of postrevolutionary Iran, while also supplying Iran in the murky "arms for hostages" Iran-Contra affair.

Such heavy-handed intervention helped create the intense anti-

Westernism that today underlies both Sunni and Shia radicalism. The fear and resentment of manipulation by the West were expressed in best-selling fashion by Iranian cultural critic Jalal Al-e Ahmad, whose 1962 book *Gharbʒadegi*—"Occidentosis," or "Westoxification"—saw Western cultural and financial dominance as a fatal disease that had to be rooted out of the Iranian body politic and by extension out of Islam as a whole. Ahmad's call was taken up across the Shia-Sunni divide by Egyptian radical ideologue Sayyid Qutb, who helped lay the groundwork for modern Islamism. In his 1964 book *Milestones,* Qutb wrote that "setting up the kingdom of God on earth and eliminating the kingdom of man means taking power from the hands of the human usurpers and restoring it to God alone"—a deliberate echo of "Judgment belongs to God alone," the seventh-century rallying cry of the *khariji* Rejectionists who assassinated Ali.

Sunni and Shia radicals alike called on a potent blend of the seventh century and the twentieth: on the Karbala story and on anti-Westernism. By the 1980s such calls were a clear danger signal to the pro-American Saudis, who were highly aware that radical Sunni energies could come home to roost in an Arabian equivalent of the Iranian Revolution. Their answer, in effect, was to deal with radical Islamism by financing it abroad, thus deflecting its impact at home. The Saudis became major exporters of Wahhabi extremism and its bitterly anti-Shia stance, from Africa to Indonesia, countering a newly strengthened sense of Shia identity and power—"the Shia revival," as it's been called—energized by the Iranian Revolution. The Sunni-Shia split had again become as politicized as when it began.

In such a confrontation, the Sunnis would seem to have a clear advantage since the Shia are only some fifteen percent of all Muslims worldwide. But raw numbers can be misleading. In the Middle East heartland of Islam, the Shia are closer to fifty percent, and wherever oil reserves are richest—Iran, Iraq, and the Persian Gulf coast, including eastern Saudi Arabia—they are in the majority. So long as oil dominates the world economy, the stakes are again as high as they were at the height of the Muslim empire. And the main issue is again what it was in the seventh century—who should lead Islam?—now played out on an international level. Where Ali once struggled against Muawiya, Shia Iran and Sunni Saudi Arabia today vie with each other for influence and political leadership of the Islamic world, a power struggle demonstrated most painfully in the cities of Iraq and in the mountains of Afghanistan and Pakistan.

As the United States has at last recognized, with thousands of American troops killed in Iraq and Afghanistan, Westerners enter such a power struggle at their own peril, all the more since many in the Middle East suspect that Western powers have deliberately manipulated the Shia-Sunni split all along in order to serve their own interests. The chaos unleashed by the invasion of Iraq in 2003 may have resulted in yet another unintended consequence in American eyes, but it was not so unintended in Iraqi eyes. "The invader has separated us," declared Muqtada al-Sadr in 2007. "Unity is power, and division is weakness."

The idea of *fitna* has now achieved yet another level of meaning, and a still more incendiary one: discord and civil war within Islam manipulated from without, deliberately fostered by enemies of Islam in order to turn Muslims against one another and thus weaken them.

This may be giving Western powers credit for more understanding than they have ever demonstrated, but if they have indeed tried to exploit division, the attempt has only rebounded against them. By now it is clear that anyone so rash as to think it possible to intervene in the Sunni-Shia split and come away unscathed is at best indulging in wishful thinking. It may be tempting to imagine that if the Bush administration had known the power of the Karbala story, American troops would never have been ordered anywhere within a hundred miles of the holy cities of Najaf and Karbala, but that too is wishful thinking. As with Yazid in the seventh century, so with George Bush in the twenty-first, history is often made by the heedless.

After close to a century of failed intervention, Westerners finally need to stand back, to acknowledge the emotive depth of the Sunni-Shia split and to accord it the respect it demands. The Karbala story has endured and strengthened not least because it reaches deep into questions of morality—of idealism versus pragmatism, purity versus compromise. Its DNA is the very stuff that tests both politics and faith and animates the vast and often terrifying arena in which the two intersect. But whether sacredness inheres in the Prophet's blood family, as the Shia believe, or in the community as a whole, as Sunnis believe, nobody in the West should forget that what unites the two main branches of Islam is far greater than what divides them, and that the vast majority of all Muslims still cherish the ideal of unity preached by Muhammad himself—an ideal the more deeply held for being so deeply broken.

Acknowledgments

This book had its origins in a series of conversations with the writer Jonathan Raban, and I am immensely grateful for his continuing interest in it and for the contribution of his fine, sharp mind in comments on the manuscript.

I am also grateful to Wilferd Madelung, Laudian Professor of Arabic at the University of Oxford, England, for his early encouragement, and to Ingvild Flaskerud of the Centre for Peace Studies at the University of Tromsö, Norway, for generously sharing her research.

Deep thanks to Stephen Rubin at Random House for his wholehearted support, to my editor, Kris Puopolo, at Doubleday for her advocacy of this book and for her splendidly acute editorial eye, and, as always, to my great friend and agent, Gloria Loomis.

Most of all, I am indebted to a man I never met and never could have: the famed Islamic historian Abu Jafar Muhammad ibn Jarir al-Tabari, who died in Baghdad in the year 923. Without his magisterial work, this book could never have been written.

Notes

Chapter 1

12   *the price of revelation*: For discussion of Islamic theologians on Muhammad's late-life childlessness, see Madelung, *Succession to Muhammad*.

16   "*Oh God, have pity on those who succeed me*": Shia *hadith* quoted by, among others, Ayatollah Khomeini. See Khomeini, *Islam and Revolution*.

Chapter 3

33   *brightly colored posters*: Popular Shia religious posters are reproduced in Steven Vincent's article "Every Land Is Karbala: In Shiite Posters, a Fever Dream for Iraq," in the May 2005 issue of *Harper's,* and can also be seen in news photos, such as that by Shawn Baldwin for *The New York Times,* December 28, 2006, "Posters of Shiite religious figures and Iranian and Syrian leaders," accompanying the article "Iran's Strong Ties with Syria."

35   "*I am from Ali and Ali is from me*": This and other statements of Muhammad on Ali are examined in, among others, Momen, *Introduction to Shi'i Islam* and Jafri, *Origins and Early Development*.

40   *People of the Cloak*: See Jafri, *Origins and Early Development* and Momen, *Introduction to Shi'i Islam*.

41   *Nahj al-Balagha*: Translated into English by Sayed Ali Reza as *Nahjul Balagha = Peak of Eloquence: Sermons, Letters and Sayings of Imam Ali ibn Abu Talib* (Bombay: Imam Foundation, 1989). Shia scholars refer to this collection as "the brother of the Quran."

44   *Al-Fahisha*: This usage is discussed in Spellberg, *Politics, Gender, and the Islamic Past* and noted in Fischer, *Iran: From Religious Dispute to Revolution.*

Chapter 4

51   *time and place . . . not in dispute*: Jafri, in *Origins and Early Development*, notes that although Ibn Ishaq, al-Tabari, and Ibn Saad did not record the events at Ghadir Khumm, "as far as the authenticity of the event itself is concerned, it has hardly ever been questioned or denied even by the most conservative Sunni authorities, who have themselves recorded it." Jafri gives details of those records.

55   *but on Ali's*: Madelung, *Succession to Muhammad* and Jafri, *Origins and Early Development* both discuss this tradition, citing Ibn Saad, *Tabaqat.*

PART TWO: ALI

Chapter 6

75   *severed head of Hussein*: This tradition is reported in Halm, *Shi'a Islam.*

76   *halal*: Though this word is generally known in the West only as it applies to Islamic dietary laws, it is used throughout Arabic-speaking countries for anything licit or permitted under Islamic law.

80   *"tribal imperative to conquest"*: See, for instance, "Tribal states must conquer to survive," on p. 243 of Patricia Crone's controversial *Meccan Trade and the Rise of Islam* (Princeton: Princeton University Press, 1987). A more nuanced look at the "tribal imperative" is in Berkey, *Formation of Islam.*

Chapter 7

88   *"goat's fart"*: Madelung, *Succession to Muhammad*, citing Ibn Asakir's twelfth-century *Tarikh Madinat Dimashq* (History of the State of Damascus).

96   *"millstone around his feet"*: Madelung, *Succession to Muhammad*, citing al-Baladhuri, *Ansab al-Ashraf* (Lineage of the Nobles).

Chapter 9

124   *"one of nine stuffed beds"*: Madelung, *Succession to Muhammad*, citing Shia *hadith* from al-Majlisi, *Bihar al-Anwar* (Ocean of Light).

Chapter 10

127   *"a bubbling spring in an easy land"*: This and other sayings of Muawiya on the exercise of power in Humphreys, *Muawiya*, citing al-Baladhuri, *Ansab al-Ashraf* (Lineage of the Nobles).

134   *"will you be cuckolds?"*: Rogerson, *Heirs of the Prophet*, citing al-Waqidi's eighth-century *Kitab al-Tarikh wa al-Maghazi* (Book of History and Campaigns).

135   "*I see Syria loathing the reign of Iraq*": Madelung, *Succession to Muhammad*, cit-
       ing al-Minqari's *Waqiat Siffin* (The Confrontation at Siffin).

135   "*you had to be led to the oath of allegiance*": Madelung, *Succession to Muham-
       mad*, citing al-Baladhuri, *Ansab al-Ashraf* (Lineage of the Nobles).

Chapter 11

149   *Ibn Washiya's* Book on Poisons: This fascinating and immensely detailed book
       is translated in full in Levey, *Medieval Arabic Toxicology.*

150   "*So was your brother cooked*": Abbott, *Aisha*, citing Ibn al-Athir's thirteenth-
       century *Al Kamil fi al-Tarikh* (The Complete History).

PART THREE: HUSSEIN

Chapter 12

168   *The hand that slipped the fatal powder*: Madelung, *Succession to Muhammad* cites
       several early historians, both Sunni and Shia, on Jaada's role, noting that al-
       Tabari suppressed the incident for political reasons.

169   "*a woman who poisons her husband?*": Madelung, *Succession to Muhammad*, cit-
       ing al-Baladhuri, *Ansab al-Ashraf* (Lineage of the Nobles).

170   "*never any subject I wished closed*": Abbott, *Aisha*, citing Ibn al-Jawzi, *Tahqiq*,
       twelfth-century Sunni collection of *hadith.*

171   "*your death as the most infamous act of Ali*": Abbott, *Aisha*, citing Ibn al-Athir's
       thirteenth-century *Al Kamil fi al-Tarikh* (The Complete History).

Chapter 13

188   *A vast cycle of* taziya: Most of the *taẓiya* Passion plays are based on al-Kashifi's
       tenth-century *Rawdat al-Shuhada* (Garden of the Martyrs), discussed in
       Halm, *Shi'a Islam* and Momen, *Introduction to Shi'i Islam*. See also Pinault,
       Horse of Karbala on both *Rawdat al-Shuhada* and al-Majlisi's seventeenth-
       century *Bihar al-Anwar* (Ocean of Light).

189   *build the wedding canopy*: Ingvild Flaskerud's DVD *Standard-Bearers of Hus-
       sein* includes rare footage of women commemorating Karbala.

Chapter 14

196   "*the Karbala factor*": Momen, *Introduction to Shi'i Islam*. Michael Fischer refers
       to it as "the Karbala paradigm."

197   "*Let the blood-stained banners of Ashura*": See Khomeini, *Islam and Revolution.*

202   *the Mahdi*: It should be noted that the term "Mahdi" is also used in Sunni Islam
       but not for a specific figure. Sunnis use it to refer to an ideal Islamic leader, and
       indeed many have claimed the title, over the centuries. In Shia Islam, however,
       there is only one Mahdi, the twelfth Imam, a clear messianic figure.

202   *eleventh-century treatise*: See al-Mufid, *The Book of Guidance,* and discussion of signs of the Mahdi's return in Sachedina, *Islamic Messianism.*

Chapter 15

209   *"the Shia revival"*: Most notably in Nasr, *The Shia Revival.*

Sources

EARLY ISLAMIC SOURCES

The source I have relied on most heavily is al-Tabari (839–923), generally acknowledged throughout the Muslim world as the most prestigious and authoritative early Islamic historian. His monumental work *Tarikh al-rusul wa-al-muluk* (History of the Prophets and Kings) starts with biblical peoples and prophets, continues with the legendary and factual history of ancient Persia, then moves on to cover in immense and intimate detail the rise of Islam and the history of the Islamic world through to the early tenth century. It has been translated into English in a magnificent project overseen by general editor Ehsan Yar-Shater and published in thirty-nine annotated volumes between the years 1985 and 1999 as *The History of al-Tabari*. Specific volumes are cited below. Al-Tabari is the source of all direct quotes and dialogue in this book unless otherwise stated in the text itself or in the Notes before this section.

The *Tarikh* is outstanding for both its breadth and its depth, as well as its style. Al-Tabari—his full name was Abu Jafar Muhammad ibn Jarir al-Tabari, but he was known simply as al-Tabari after his birthplace in Tabaristan, on the southern shore of the Caspian Sea—was a

Sunni scholar living and writing in the Abbasid capital of Baghdad. His work is so inclusive as to make extremist Sunnis suspicious that he may have had "Shia sympathies." He made extensive use of oral history, traveling throughout the empire to record interviews and documenting them in detail so that the chain of communication was clear, always leading back to an eyewitness to the events in question. The *Tarikh* thus has an immediacy that Westerners tend not to associate with classic histories. Voices from the seventh century—not only those of the people being interviewed but also those of the people they are talking about, whom they often quote verbatim—seem to speak directly to the reader. The result is so vivid that you can almost hear the inflections in their voices and see their gestures as they speak. All other early Islamic histories seem somewhat dry by comparison.

Al-Tabari combined these oral accounts with earlier written histories, fully acknowledging his debt at every step. He did this so faithfully and skillfully that his own work soon superseded some of his written sources, which were no longer copied or saved. His detailed account of what happened at Karbala in the year 680, for instance, is based in large part on *Kitab Maqtal al-Hussein* (The Book of the Murder of Hussein), written by the Kufan Abu Mikhnaf just fifty years after Karbala from firsthand eyewitness accounts, including that of Hussein's one surviving son.

For anyone who delights in the Middle Eastern style of narrative, al-Tabari is a joy to read, though Western readers accustomed to tight structure and a clear authorial point of view may be disconcerted at first. Sometimes the same event or conversation is told from more than a dozen points of view, and the narrative thread weaves back and forth in time, with each separate account adding to the ones that came before, but from a slightly different angle. This use of multiple voices creates an almost postmodern effect; what seems at first to be lack of structure slowly reveals itself as a vast edifice of brilliant structural integrity.

Given his method, it should come as no surprise that some of the dialogue quoted in the present book is given several times in al-Tabari, as recounted by different witnesses and sources. While the general drift of these accounts is usually the same, the wording obviously differs according to who is speaking, as do the details: one person remembers this detail; another, that. My sole criterion in deciding which of multiple versions of a quote to use was the desire for clarity, eschewing more ornate and worked-over versions for clearer, more direct ones and opting for detail over generality.

Where al-Tabari offers conflicting versions of an event from different sources, I have noted the difference and followed his example in reserving judgment. "In everything which I mention herein," he writes in the introduction to the *Tarikh*, "I rely only on established [written] reports, which I identify, and on [oral] accounts, which I ascribe by name to their transmitters . . . Knowledge is only obtained by the statements of reporters and transmitters, not by rational deduction or by intuitive inference. And if we have mentioned in this book any report about certain men of the past which the reader finds objectionable or the hearer offensive . . . he should know that this has not come about on our account, but on account of one of those who has transmitted it to us, and that we have presented it only in the way in which it was presented to us."

I have made especially heavy use of the following volumes:

The Foundation of the Community, tr. and annotated W. Montgomery Watt and M. V. McDonald, Vol. VII. Albany: State University of New York Press, 1987.

The Victory of Islam, tr. and annotated Michael Fishbein, Vol. VIII. Albany: State University of New York Press, 1997.

The Last Years of the Prophet, tr. and annotated Ismail K. Poonawala, Vol. IX. Albany: State University of New York Press, 1990.

The Crisis of the Early Caliphate, tr. and annotated R. Stephen Humphreys, Vol. XV. Albany: State University of New York Press, 1990.

The Community Divided: The Caliphate of Ali, tr. and annotated Adrian Brockett, Vol. XVI. Albany: State University of New York Press, 1997.

The First Civil War: From the Battle of Siffin to the Death of Ali, tr. and annotated G. R. Hawting, Vol. XVII. Albany: State University of New York Press, 1996.

Between Civil Wars: The Caliphate of Muawiyah, tr. and annotated Michael G. Morony, Vol. XVIII. Albany: State University of New York Press, 1987.

The Caliphate of Yazid b. Muawiyah, tr. and annotated I. K. A. Howard, Vol. XIX. Albany: State University of New York Press, 1990.

The earliest biography of Muhammad is that of Ibn Ishaq, whose *Sirat Rasul Allah* (Life of the Messenger of God) is the basis of all subsequent biographies of the Prophet. Like al-Tabari's work, it is regarded as authoritative throughout the Muslim world, and al-Tabari drew on it heavily for his own account of Muhammad's life.

Muhammad ibn Ishaq was born in Medina around the year 704 and died in Baghdad in 767. His original manuscript no longer exists, since it was superseded by an expanded and annotated version by the Basra-born historian Ibn Hisham, who lived and worked in Egypt. Ibn Hisham's version of Ibn Ishaq's biography has been translated into English as *The Life of Muhammad: A Translation of Ibn Ishaq's Sirat Rasul Allah*, tr. Alfred Guillaume (Oxford: Oxford University Press, 1955).

Two other early Islamic historians demand special note. The work of al-Baladhuri complements that of al-Tabari. Born in Persia, Ahmad ibn Yahya al-Baladhuri lived and worked in Baghdad, where he died in 892. His *Kitab Futuh al-Buldan* (Book of the Conquests of Lands) has been translated by Philip Hitti and Francis C. Murgotten as *The Origins of the Islamic State* (New York: Columbia University Press, 1916–24). His *Ansab al-Ashraf* (Lineage of the Nobles), which covers the reigns of the early caliphs and includes thousands of capsule biographies, is not yet available in English translation.

Muhammad ibn Sa'd (spelled "Saad" in this book) was one of the earliest compilers of biographies of major figures in early Islam, and his work proved a major source for later historians, including al-Tabari. Born in Basra in 764, he lived in Baghdad, where he died in 845. Abridged selections from two volumes of his nine-volume collection

Kitab al-Tabaqat al-Kabir (Great Book of Generations) can be found in *The Women of Madina*, tr. Aisha Bewley (London: Ta-Ha Publishers, 1995) and *The Men of Madina*, tr. Aisha Bewley (London: Ta-Ha Publishers, 1997).

I have worked with three English versions of the Quran (I use the word "version" rather than "translation" since a basic tenet of Islam is that the Quran as the word of God cannot be translated, only "interpreted" in other languages):

The Koran, tr. Edward H. Palmer. Oxford: Clarendon Press, 1900.

The Koran Interpreted, tr. A. J. Arberry. New York: Macmillan, 1955.

The Koran, tr. N. J. Dawood. London: Penguin, 1956.

CONTEMPORARY SOURCES

This book is especially indebted to the work of the following scholars, listed here by area of expertise.

The Early Caliphate

Wilferd Madelung's *The Succession to Muhammad: A Study of the Early Caliphate* (Cambridge: Cambridge University Press, 1997) is a magisterial study of the caliphates of Abu Bakr, Omar, Othman, and Ali, based on close reading of original sources. Extensively and fascinatingly footnoted, it emphasizes Ali's claim to the succession.

Marshall G. S. Hodgson's *The Venture of Islam: Conscience and History in a World Civilization* is a three-volume study of the historical development of Islamic civilization, with numerous tables of time lines. *The Classical Age of Islam*, Vol. 1 (Chicago: University of Chicago Press, 1961) covers the rise of Muhammad to the year 945.

W. Montgomery Watt's *The Formative Period of Islamic Thought* (Edinburgh: Edinburgh University Press, 1973) examines developments within Islam from the *khariji* Rejectionists to the establishment of Sunnism.

Shia Islam

S. H. M. Jafri's *The Origins and Early Development of Shi'a Islam* (London: Longman, 1979) provides a detailed and deeply sympathetic examination of Shia history and theology from the time of Muhammad through to the twelve Imams.

Vali Nasr's *The Shia Revival: How Conflicts Within Islam Will Shape the Future* (New York: Norton, 2006) is an excellent and highly readable overview of the Shia-Sunni conflict in the twentieth century and into the twenty-first.

Moojan Momen's *An Introduction to Shi'i Islam: The History and Doctrines of Twelver Shi'ism* (New Haven: Yale University Press, 1985) is far more detailed than one might expect an "introduction" to be, and is especially good on Shia theology.

The Iranian Revolution

Anthropologist Michael M. Fischer's work, in particular *Iran: From Religious Dispute to Revolution* (Cambridge: Harvard University Press, 1980), is outstanding. Also his essay "The Iranian Revolution: Five Frames for Understanding," in *Critical Moments in Religious History*, ed. Kenneth Keulman (Macon, Ga.: Mercer University Press, 1993) and, in collaboration with Mehdi Abedi, *Debating Muslims: Cultural Dialogues in Postmodernity and Tradition* (Madison: University of Wisconsin Press, 1990).

Nikki Keddie's *Modern Iran: Roots and Results of Revolution* (New Haven: Yale University Press, 2003) is rightfully regarded as essential reading, as should be almost all the essays in an anthology edited by Keddie: *Religion and Politics in Iran: Shi'ism from Quietism to Revolution* (New Haven: Yale University Press, 1983).

Ali Shariati's lectures can be found in translation at www.shariati .com. His most influential lectures have been published in English as *What Is to Be Done: The Enlightened Thinkers and an Islamic Renaissance*

(Houston: Institute for Research and Islamic Studies, 1986) and as *Red Shi'ism* (Teheran: Hamdani Foundation, 1979). His lectures on Hussein and martyrdom can be found in *Jihad and Shahadat: Struggle and Martyrdom in Islam,* ed. Mehdi Abedi and Gary Legenhausen (North Haledon, N.J.: Islamic Publications International, 1986).

Ashura Rituals and Karbala Imagery

Peter J. Chelkowski, editor of *Ta'ziyeh: Ritual and Drama in Iran* (New York: New York University Press, 1979), provides invaluable insight into both the content and import of Karbala Passion plays, while *Staging a Revolution: The Art of Persuasion in the Islamic Republic of Iran,* by Chelkowski and Hamid Dabashi (New York: New York University Press, 1999), is a superb visual survey and analysis of the collective symbols used in the Iranian Revolution and the subsequent war with Iraq.

David Pinault provides on-the-ground understanding of the emotive and theological power of the Karbala story in *The Shiites: Ritual and Popular Piety in a Muslim Community* (New York: St. Martin's Press, 1992) and in *Horse of Karbala: Muslim Devotional Life in India* (New York: Palgrave, 2001).

Kamran Scot Aghaie's detailed work on Shia symbolism and ritual can be found in *The Martyrs of Karbala: Shi'i Symbols and Rituals in Modern Iran* (Seattle: University of Washington Press, 2004) and *The Women of Karbala: Ritual Performance and Symbolic Discourses in Modern Shi'i Islam* (Austin: University of Texas Press, 2005).

Aisha

Nabia Abbott's *Aishah: The Beloved of Muhammad* (Chicago: University of Chicago Press, 1942) is the classic biography in English, drawing on the earliest Islamic histories and in particular on al-Tabari, Ibn Saad, and al-Baladhuri.

Denise A. Spellberg's *Politics, Gender, and the Islamic Past: The Legacy of Aisha bint Abu Bakr* (New York: Columbia University Press,

1994) provides a detailed exploration of the multiple ways in which Aisha has been perceived and interpreted over the centuries, both positively and negatively.

The following is a select bibliography of additional books that have been particularly helpful in both specific details and general background:

Ahmed, Leila. *Women and Gender in Islam*. New Haven: Yale University Press, 1992.

Ajami, Fouad. *The Vanished Imam: Musa al Sadr and the Shia of Lebanon*. Ithaca: Cornell University Press, 1986.

————. *The Foreigner's Gift: The Americans, the Arabs, and the Iraqis in Iraq*. New York: Free Press, 2006.

Akhavi, Shahrough. "Shariati's Social Thought." In *Religion and Politics in Iran*, ed. Nikki Keddie. New Haven: Yale University Press, 1983.

Al-e Ahmad, Jalal. *Occidentosis: A Plague from the West*, tr. R. Campbell from the 1962 Farsi *Gharbzadegi*. Berkeley: Mizan Press, 1984.

Allen, Charles. *God's Terrorists: The Wahhabi Cult and the Hidden Roots of Modern Jihad*. Cambridge: Da Capo, 2006.

Al-Mufid, Shaykh. *The Book of Guidance into the Lives of the Twelve Imams*, tr. I. K. A. Howard of *Kitab al-Irshad*. London: Muhammadi Trust, 1981.

Arjomand, Said Amir. *The Shadow of God and the Hidden Imam: Religion, Political Order and Societal Change in Shi'ite Iran from the Beginning to 1890*. Chicago: University of Chicago Press, 1984.

Aslan, Reza. *No God but God: The Origins, Evolution, and Future of Islam*. New York: Random House, 2005.

Ayoub, Mahmoud. *Redemptive Suffering in Islam: A Study of the Devotional Aspects of Ashura*. The Hague: Mouton, 1978.

Beeman, William O. "Images of the Great Satan: Representations of the United States in the Iranian Revolution." In *Religion and Politics in Iran*, ed. Nikki Keddie. New Haven: Yale University Press, 1983.

Berkey, Jonathan P. *The Formation of Islam: Religion and Society in the Near East, 600–1800*. Cambridge: Cambridge University Press, 2003.

Cockburn, Patrick. *Muqtada: Muqtada al-Sadr, the Shia Revival, and the Struggle for Iraq*. New York: Scribner, 2008.

Cole, Juan. *Sacred Space and Holy War: The Politics, Culture and History of Shi'ite Islam*. London: I. B. Tauris, 2002.

————. Ongoing informed commentary on Middle Eastern politics at www
.juancole.com.

Cole, Juan, and Nikki Keddie, eds. *Shi'ism and Social Protest*. New Haven: Yale University Press, 1986.

Cook, David. *Understanding Jihad*. Berkeley: University of California Press, 2005.

Crone, Patricia, and Martin Hinds. *God's Caliph: Religious Authority in the First Centuries of Islam*. Cambridge: Cambridge University Press, 1986.

Dodge, Toby. *Inventing Iraq: The Failure of Nation Building and a History Denied*. New York: Columbia University Press, 2003.

Enayat, Hamid. *Modern Islamic Political Thought*. London: I. B. Tauris, 2005.

Flaskerud, Ingvild. *Standard-Bearers of Hussein: Women Commemorating Karbala*. DVD for academic and research distribution only. ingvildf@sv.uit.no, University of Tromsö, 2003.

Geertz, Clifford. *Islam Observed: Religious Development in Morocco and Indonesia*. Chicago: University of Chicago Press, 1968.

————. *The Interpretation of Cultures: Selected Essays*. New York: Basic Books, 1973.

Grant, Christina Phelps. *The Syrian Desert: Caravans, Travel and Exploration*. London: A. and C. Black, 1937.

Halm, Heinz. *Shi'a Islam: From Religion to Revolution*. Princeton: Markus Wiener, 1997.

Heck, Gene W. "Arabia Without Spices." In *Journal of the American Oriental Society*, vol. 123. 2003.

Hegland, Mary. "Two Images of Husain: Accommodation and Revolution in an Iranian Village." In *Religion and Politics in Iran*, ed. Nikki Keddie. New Haven: Yale University Press, 1983.

Hjarpe, Jan. "The Ta'ziya Ecstasy as Political Expression." In *Religious Ecstasy*, ed. Nils G. Holm. Stockholm: Almqvist and Wiksell, 1982.

Hourani, Albert. *A History of the Arab Peoples*. Cambridge: Harvard University Press, 1991.

Humphreys, R. Stephen. *Islamic History: A Framework for Inquiry*. Minneapolis: Biblioteca Islamica, 1988.

———. *Mu'awiya ibn Abu Sufyan: From Arabia to Empire*. Oxford: One World, 2006.

Kennedy, Hugh. *The Prophet and the Age of the Caliphates: The Islamic Near East from the Sixth to the Eleventh Century*. London: Longman, 1986.

———. *The Great Arab Conquests: How the Spread of Islam Changed the World We Live In*. Cambridge: Da Capo, 2008.

Kenney, Jeffrey T. *Muslim Rebels: Kharijites and the Politics of Extremism in Egypt*. Oxford: Oxford University Press, 2006.

Khomeini, Ruhollah. *Islam and Revolution: Writings and Declarations of Imam Khomeini*, tr. Hamid Algar. Berkeley: Mizan Press, 1981.

Kurzman, Charles. *The Unthinkable Revolution in Iran*. Cambridge: Harvard University Press, 2004.

Lammens, Henri. "Fatima and the Daughters of Muhammad." In *The Quest for the Historical Muhammad*, ed. Ibn Warraq. Amherst: Prometheus Books, 2000.

Levey, Martin. *Early Arabic Pharmacology*. Leiden: E. J. Brill, 1973.

———. *Medieval Arabic Toxicology: The "Book on Poisons" of Ibn Wahshiya and Its Relation to Early Indian and Greek Texts*. Philadelphia: American Philosophical Society, 1966.

Lewis, David Levering. *God's Crucible: Islam and the Making of Europe*. New York: Norton, 2008.

Mernissi, Fatima. *The Veil and the Male Elite: A Feminist Interpretation of Women's Rights in Islam*. New York: Basic Books, 1991.

———. *The Forgotten Queen of Islam*. Oxford: Oxford University Press, 1993.

Moin, Baqer. *Khomeini: Life of the Ayatollah*. New York: Thomas Dunne, 1999.

Morony, Michael G. *Iraq After the Muslim Conquest*. Princeton: Princeton University Press, 1984.

Motahhary, Morteza. *The Martyr*. Houston: Free Islamic Literatures, 1980.

Mottahedeh, Roy. *The Mantle of the Prophet: Religion and Politics in Iran*. Oxford: One World, 1985.

Musil, Alois. *The Middle Euphrates: A Topographical Itinerary*. New York: American Geographical Society, 1927.

———. *The Manners and Customs of the Rwala Bedouins*. New York: American Geographical Society, 1928.

Nakash, Yitzhak. *Reaching for Power: The Shi'a in the Modern Arab World*. Princeton: Princeton University Press, 2006.

————. *The Shi'is of Iraq*. Princeton: Princeton University Press, 1994.

Packer, George. *The Assassins' Gate*. New York: Farrar, Straus and Giroux, 2005.

Pelly, Lewis. *The Miracle Play of Hasan and Hussein, Collected from Oral Tradition*. London: W. H. Allen, 1879.

Qutb, Sayyid. *Milestones [Ma'alim f'il-Tariq*, 1964]. Karachi: International Islamic Publishers, 1981.

Rahnema, Ali. *An Islamic Utopian: A Political Biography of Ali Shariati*. London: I. B. Tauris, 1998.

Richard, Yann. *Shi'ite Islam: Polity, Ideology, and Creed*. Oxford: Blackwell, 1995.

Robinson, Chase F. *Islamic Historiography*. Cambridge: Cambridge University Press, 2003.

Rodinson, Maxime. *Muhammad*. New York: Pantheon, 1971.

Rogerson, Barnaby. *The Heirs of the Prophet Muhammad*. London: Little, Brown, 2006.

Rosen, Nir. *In the Belly of the Green Bird: The Triumph of the Martyrs in Iraq*. New York: Free Press, 2006.

Ruthven, Malise. *Islam in the World*. Oxford: Oxford University Press, 2000.

Sachedina, Adulaziz Abdulhussein. *Islamic Messianism: The Idea of Mahdi in Twelver Shiism*. Albany: State University of New York Press, 1981.

Shadid, Anthony. *Night Draws Near: Iraq's People in the Shadow of America's War*. New York: Henry Holt, 2005.

Stark, Freya. *Baghdad Sketches*. New York: Dutton, 1938.

————. *East Is West*. London: John Murray, 1945.

Taheri, Amir. *The Spirit of Allah: Khomeini and the Islamic Revolution*. Bethesda: Adler and Adler, 1986.

————. *Holy Terror: The Inside Story of Islamic Terrorism*. London: Hutchinson, 1987.

Thaiss, Gustav. "Religious Symbolism and Social Change: The Drama of Hussein." In *Scholars, Saints, and Sufis: Muslim Religious Institutions in the Middle East Since 1500*, ed. Nikki Keddie. Berkeley: University of California Press, 1972.

————. "Unity and Discord: The Symbol of Husayn in Iran." In *Iranian Civilization and Culture*, ed. Charles J. Adams. Montreal: McGill University Institute of Islamic Studies, 1972.

Watt, W. Montgomery. *Muhammad at Mecca*. Oxford: Oxford University Press, 1953.

————. *Muhammad at Medina*. Oxford: Oxford University Press, 1956.

————. "The Significance of the Early Stages of Imami Shi'ism." In *Religion and Politics in Iran*, ed. Nikki Keddie. New Haven: Yale University Press, 1983.

Young, Gavin. *Iraq: Land of Two Rivers*. London: Collins, 1980.

Zakaria, Rafiq. *The Struggle Within Islam: The Conflict Between Religion and Politics*. London: Penguin, 1988.

Index